T0339488

Determining Leadership Potential

We are in the midst of a leadership crisis that is derailing business success, and it's time to get rigorous about talent. This book will show you how, with an effective and consistent framework, to help galvanize decision-makers around leadership potential.

Time and time again, organizations place too many leaders in roles they are not a good fit for. The financial, strategic, and human costs of poor leadership are staggering and unnecessary. But organizations that effectively identify high-potential talent are likely to financially outperform those that do not do this work by a factor of 4.2 to 1, not to mention all the other positive impacts. Backed by the authors' research, including a study with 50+ global CEOs, the insights and strategies packed into this book will help you eliminate the shocking variation that exists in how people think about determining leadership potential – and empower decision-makers to be game-changers to optimize their organizations.

For too long, leadership potential has been treated as an imprecise art and inconsistently applied. CEOs, board members, senior managers, and HR professionals will welcome the thought-provoking insights and practical tools this book gives to build a pipeline of strong leaders.

Dr. Kimberly Janson is a 25+-year talent and organizational development executive working in 40+ countries, with 300+ companies. As CEO of Janson Associates and founder of Legacy Farms, she has been named a Top 10 Thought Leader and Top 10 Executive Coach in 2021. Working with C-suite leaders, teams, businesses, and individuals, Kim enables change to achieve stellar business results. Kim also authored *Demystifying Talent Management*, winner of the Axion Book Award.

Dr. Melody Rawlings is a business professor, doctoral chair, and director of the Center for the Advancement of Virtual Organizations at Northcentral University. She has led remote teams for 10+ years and is a frequent presenter at international conferences. She has developed partnerships between corporations and higher ed, and has managed her own business. Melody has authored peer-reviewed publications on leadership topics and has taught internationally in Europe and Asia.

Determining Leadership Potential

Powerful Insights to Winning at the Talent Game

Dr. Kimberly Janson and
Dr. Melody Rawlings

 Routledge
Taylor & Francis Group

NEW YORK AND LONDON

Cover image: Hannah Janson

First published 2022
by Routledge
605 Third Avenue, New York, NY 10158

and by Routledge
4 Park Square, Milton Park, Abingdon, Oxon, OX14 4RN

Routledge is an imprint of the Taylor & Francis Group, an informa business

Library of Congress Cataloging-in-Publication Data
Names: Janson, Kimberly, author. | Rawlings, Melody, author.
Title: Determining leadership potential : powerful insights to winning at the talent game / Kimberly Janson and Melody Rawlings.
Description: 1 Edition. | New York, NY : Routledge, 2022. | Includes bibliographical references and index. |
Identifiers: LCCN 2022007128 | ISBN 9781032223469 (hardback) | ISBN 9781032220338 (paperback) | ISBN 9781003272212 (ebook)
Subjects: LCSH: Leadership. | Executive ability. | Emotional intelligence. Decision making.
Classification: LCC HD57.7 .J357 2022 | DDC 658.4/092–dc23/eng/20220323
LC record available at https://lccn.loc.gov/2022007128

ISBN: 978-1-032-22346-9 (hbk)
ISBN: 978-1-032-22033-8 (pbk)
ISBN: 978-1-003-27221-2 (ebk)

DOI: 10.4324/9781003272212

Typeset in Sabon
by Deanta Global Publishing Services, Chennai, India

DETERMINING LEADERSHIP POTENTIAL

Kim's Dedication

This book is dedicated to my husband, Mike Janson. He's the magic that allows everything to happen. I knew what I was doing New Year's Eve in 1989 when I sent him that shot of Wild Turkey. Best decision I have ever made. I tell him I married for looks but, in truth, I married for life. Thank you for all you do for us and for all you do to enable me to be me.

Melody's Dedication

To my husband and best friend, Steven Rawlings, who is always my greatest source of support and encouragement! Thank you for being my inspiration and rock of strength! This book is also dedicated to my daughters, Meredith Rawlings and Kaitlyn Rawlings Locco, my greatest cheerleaders, and excellent proofreaders. You both are my inspiration!

Table of Contents

Contributor

Dani Monroe, guest co-author for Chapter 2, "Bias and Determining Leadership Potential," is the founder of MV CDO Summit and President of CenterFocus International, Inc., USA. She has led the Csuites of Fortune 100 companies to success in global diversity, inclusion, and organization effectiveness – favorably impacting their bottom line, reputation, and business potential. With a 20+-year career, she has brought definition and depth to the dialogue about diversity and set the pace for change and precedence in strategies of global diversity and inclusion. She designed and facilitated *organizational* change strategies that integrated all components for the diversity and inclusion strategy – from metrics and accountability for senior leaders to leadership curriculum and inclusive work processes. Dani is also the author of *Untapped Talent: Unleashing the Power of the Hidden Workforce.*

Preface

Kim and Melody met when Kim was in her PhD program at Northcentral University. Melody was a professor, and it was friendship at first sight. Sharing many of the same views on talent and leadership, they bonded over ideas. They continued bonding over kids and animals. Plus...redheads unite!

This friendship, fueled by deep mutual professional respect, led Kim to ask Melody to be her Dissertation Chair. Melody, equally passionate about this pervasive issue, readily agreed. They were so intrigued by the results of the dissertation study that they quickly planned a second global study. Kim continued her work with CEOs and conducted a third study focusing just on perspectives of CEOs related to determining leadership potential. When Kim decided she was writing a book on the topic, she asked Melody to partner. Not only could the two of them produce a better result for the leaders in the business world (via Kim's corporate expertise) but perhaps they could teach more people early in their education how to do this well (via Melody's academic expertise).

Due to our deep belief in the importance of this topic and our commitment to helping you develop great competence in this area, we have produced many more resources for you and made those available free of charge at determiningleadershippotential.com

We want nothing short of changing the world with this book. Too many people head home from work feeling defeated, disenchanted, or unfulfilled because they have been impacted by someone in a leadership role who simply should not be in that role. There are many reasons why they should not be there, but the result is the same. Why don't we just do a better job when selecting leaders? Determining leadership potential demands extreme focus…right now! We are experiencing a leadership crisis around the world in so many ways.

We hope you find these insights useful and join us in ending this global talent crisis – now more than ever, we need strong leaders!

Acknowledgements

Kim's Acknowledgements

We are so blessed to have such a support system. My first thanks go to my co-author and partner-in-crime, Dr. Melody Rawlings, whose brilliance and wonderful character make me better. Special thanks go to Lisa Cohn and Ashley Brown who were early reviewers of the rough stuff. Lisa Cohn is a rock star on every level (except for her choice in football teams) in her brilliance, humor, friendship, and ninja editing skills. Ashley Brown has been a tremendous facilitator of all things relating to this book. Appreciation goes to Michelle Withers for her amazing quant skills and data mind! A heartful thanks to our research study participants, especially the 51 CEOs who spent sincere time with me to make the world better by improving our hit rate in selecting leaders. Deep gratitude to Allan Church, Head of Talent at PepsiCo, for all his brilliant work and endless patience in answering my questions. So much love and appreciation to Janson Associates clients who were steadfast in their support! We had several friends and family who reviewed the manuscript for whom we are grateful – my oldest sister Patt (not my mom's favorite...if you were wondering because I am), Virginia Sorti, my sister-in-law Anita, and my son Michael. Huge shout-out goes to my research assistant, Kaitlynn Marrese, who was a magician with data analysis, deep thinking, and of course editing. Big appreciation to Ken Lizotte, our publisher agent, who not only reviewed the manuscript but procured the book deal with Routledge in the first place!

Tremendous thanks to Dani Monroe for co-authoring the chapter on bias and continuing to be such a great role model.

In addition to being reviewers, huge thanks for the ongoing, endless support provided by my kids – Hannah (who brings amazing marketing and growth ideas all the time) and Michael (my partner in Legacy Farms), their partners, Anthony (just all-around great guy), and Dylan (who with her own PhD in neuroscience always gives good ideas)...and the person who identified the most grammatical errors, the Queen herself, my 96-year-old mother...Betty Hill.

Thanks to all the leaders and readers who have a desire to be better. We are proud to share that journey with you!

Melody's Acknowledgements

It's been an honor to co-author this book with Kim who is "a force!" It has been an amazing journey that would not have been possible had it not been for all the folks Kim acknowledged – much gratefulness to all of them! Tremendous gratitude to my husband, Steve, and daughter, Meredith, for reviewing the manuscript and providing inspiration as well as unwavering support, encouragement, and a "kick in the pants" when I needed it! A special thank-you to my dear friends Dr. Samantha Hedgspeth and Dr. Kent Tonkin for taking time to review the manuscript and provide valuable feedback. A heartfelt thank-you to you, our readers, for your interest and desire to improve how we determine leadership potential in others.

List of Acronyms

CEO	chief executive officer
CFO	chief financial officer
CHRO	chief human resource officer
C-LEVEL /	
C-SUITE	high-ranking executive titles in an organization. The letter C stands for "chief."
DLP	determining leadership potential
EI	emotional intelligence
EQ	emotional intelligence / emotional quotient
GDLP	Global Study on Determining Leadership Potential
HR	human resources
IMPL(S)	intelligence, motivation, personality, and learning agility
IP	imposter phenomenon
IQ	intelligence quotient
LB	Leadership Blueprint
LFE	learning from experience
LP	leadership potential
MBTI	Myers–Briggs Type Indicator
MTMM	multi-trait, multi-method
OCEAN	openness, conscientiousness, extraversion, agreeableness, and neuroticism
PI	predictive index
ROI	return on investment

The Potential of Potential

Kimberly Janson and Melody Rawlings

This chapter provides an in-depth discussion about the great impact a leader has on team members. It can be profound. Profoundly good…and profoundly bad. Because of this, the role of the leader is precious and sacred. Leadership should be a vocation, not a title. It takes a special person to be a leader. Everyone can readily name a leader whom they hold in high regard. It is that impact people should look to create when selecting leaders. Therefore, those of you lucky enough to be in the position of selecting people to be leaders have a tremendous responsibility. It shouldn't be just anyone who is put into a leadership role, and everyone would agree to that statement. Yet, look around. There are so many people in leadership roles that cause others to shake their head(s) and ask themselves, "how were they placed into that role and why are they allowed to stay?" Some estimates indicate the cost of a bad leader is upwards of $3 million (Buckner & Marberry, 2018). Those who are choosing leaders need a reckoning. We need to do better and be better.

We Have a Leadership Crisis at Hand

History is rich with examples of amazing leaders. These leaders have embodied the characteristics that made them excellent leaders for their people and their times. We have great leaders today, as well. Unfortunately, there are too many examples of people in leadership roles who simply should not be there. We are surrounded by inept, self-focused, under-skilled people in leadership roles. These "bad" leaders permeate every aspect of our lives: business, education, religion, sports, entertainment, government, and more.

DOI: 10.4324/9781003272212-1

Whew. This is a downer. But that doesn't mean the leadership crisis should leave us hopeless. Yes, unfortunately, there is a serious mismatch between people currently holding leadership roles and who should really be in those roles and what is needed in those roles. However, by bringing attention to the criticality of this very issue of determining leadership potential and being more aware of the devastating impact it can have when we get it wrong, we intend to fix it...and to educate and enlist you in helping to fix it.

Kim has traveled the world and worked with leaders on the ground in more than 40 countries and more than 300 companies. She's witnessed the power of great leadership and the tremendously negative impact of poor leadership. Those she has spoken to can readily share a robust story of a bad leader. Take the explosive supply chain leader in Europe who was brilliant and cared deeply but was volatile and therefore polarizing – something he simply could not or would not change. Compare that negative impact to the amazing leader in Germany (Jan Kruise, Head of Europe – FrieslandCampina) who bleeds the colors of his company to such a degree that he leaves no stone unturned while creating employee engagement, client satisfaction, and great results. The gap is tremendous between the two. We aren't speaking of leaders being poor leaders who are simply under-skilled and need coaching and development. We are speaking of people who do not have enough of the essential fundamental building blocks that will allow them to get out of their way to be strong leaders.

This crisis must be fixed. The goal should be nothing short of changing the world for the better. To make it better, we must identify the cause of the issue; we are awful at choosing leaders. So, if we want better leaders, we must get better at selecting leaders. Come on!! We are smarter than our results in the leaders we are selecting! We need to significantly raise our game in this space, and this book aims to equip you with knowledge and techniques to elevate *your* game in this work.

We have committed to getting this right for you.

We have conducted an extensive meta-analysis of the research and literature in determining leadership potential. We have spoken to subject-matter experts and have conducted three specific research studies on the topic – more details on this later. We have more than 50 years combined in global corporate and academic experience and expertise.

As a result, we will provide you with the current thought leadership combined with practical advice in order to achieve better results. Find more information, including detailed white papers on these studies, on determiningleadershippotential.com.

Top Ten Reasons We Struggle to Consistently Pick Good Leaders

To begin our understanding of how to improve our ability to determine leadership potential, we need to understand the leading reasons for this poor leadership dynamic and the headwinds we face. There are many reasons why this dynamic is "a thing." Below are the top ten reasons we have witnessed with clients and organizations in our more than 50 years of combined experience, coupled with the results of our extensive research.

1. **Variation in criteria being used.** Years' worth of expert-led academic research, extensive practitioner experience and, importantly, the results from our very own three research studies contribute to sounding the alarm on variation. Leaders at different levels in organizations use different criteria and tools to determine leadership potential. Consequently, it creates a disconnect at each level (Janson, 2020). Over time, this issue will result in a faulty pipeline of leaders. If everyone at each level is looking for something different, how in the world will companies be able to develop a set of future leaders possessing the essential capabilities?

2. **Business environment velocity.** Today's and tomorrow's leaders are challenged by a complicated, uncertain, and dynamic business environment that requires them to act with agility. Change and the speed of change are two significant contributors to an increasingly challenging business environment. While change is necessary and unending, success requires a distinct leader ready to transform businesses by effectively navigating a dynamic business environment. Therefore, leaders need to factor this reality much more into the

identification and selection process for leaders to choose leaders who can navigate this reality.

3. **Leadership development is not a panacea.** Approximately \$366 billion is spent each year globally on developing leaders. Much of that money is considered a waste for many reasons – including much of it being spent targeting the wrong people (Hieker & Pringle, 2021). A general concern about current leaders in the pipeline is that many of them are believed not to have the same level of potential. One study of three large organizations indicated that nearly half of the leaders considered high potentials were not suitable for inclusion in that pool, with approximately 12% being in the bottom quartile of leaders (Zenger & Folkman, 2018). This is true of Kim's experience in doing talent planning work in organizations around the world. Less than 10% of the people appearing on the talent plan are actually high potentials yet the initial assertions by leaders in this work are usually at the 50% mark. When Kim pushes back on specific elements of each person, their case for why the person is a great and future leader crumbles. People simply aren't skilled enough to properly make these determinations...yet! Leadership development work alone will not fix this. Needed are enough raw ingredients to work with to develop and produce high-functioning leaders.

4. **No clear framework.** Only a few companies have established clear frameworks for determining leadership potential. This lack of a clear framework can cause disconnects in how leadership potential is determined. Consequently, a gap is perpetuated at each layer of an organization because there is a lack of consistency in how leaders think about the potential. This causes too much variety in the talent pipeline – or worse still, it may result in no pipeline of talent at all.

5. **Leader selection competence varies.** A keen focus on determining leadership potential is essential because leaders are often ineffective at selecting other leaders. Despite all the evidence demonstrating the positive results by those who determine leadership potential well, many leaders are still not competent enough at selecting high-potential leaders. Many focus their efforts purely on technical skills rather than on characteristics more closely related to being high-potential leaders. The other complicating factor is that leaders think they are better at determining this potential than the results prove out.

6. **Academic research is inadequate.** There is a shortage of studies focusing only on leader selection. Academics and practitioners are pushing for more research to be conducted in this area (Ignatieva

& Babina, 2019). Many of the extant studies focus only on performance management, very specific tools, and leader behavior models. There remains a lack of guidance for practitioners about how to effectively assess potential. Researchers have had their competence challenged – often described as being out of touch with real-world needs – and the scholarship related to leadership is chaotically heterogeneous. Compounding this process is that most research on leadership potential has focused on the CEO's role, thus leaving the next level of leadership largely unstudied.

7. **Practitioners are confused and under-skilled.** Contemporary practitioners are not well-schooled in assessment or leadership fundamentals and do not make fact-based or theory-based decisions when determining potential. Frankly, so many practitioners are not only inadequate, but they also appear not to know what they are doing. Processes and templates are used to mask real depth and competence. Practitioners in organizations doing this work are accused of losing touch with the research and the science which is causing a further gap in the competence of practitioners. This is one of Kim's biggest pet peeves in working with existing HR professionals. C'mon…know your craft! Study and be proficient! Our clients depend upon us, and we hold the keys to making a true difference in organizations!

8. **Unclear ownership.** Who owns this work to determine leadership potential? Do managers? HR? Talent management professionals? Organizational development professionals? CEOs? This is another root cause of this issue. The fields of talent management (TM) and organizational development (OD) are not only relatively new to the scene but have been evolving. The implications of determining leadership potential are based on the degree of functional expertise one is working with. For example, an OD professional will view everyone as having potential, whereas a TM professional will seek to focus on only those with high potential. This fundamental difference in philosophies will then drive who has access to what, where investment dollars are spent, and ultimately how well leaders are identified and then developed.

9. **Talent shortage.** A substantial challenge in this work is that the number of people who may be considered high potential is only a small percentage of the population. Some experts (Zenger & Folkman, 2018) indicate this population constitutes approximately 5% of employees, while others, such as Church (2015) estimate it as making up 15–20% of individuals. Added to this issue is the shrinking workforce. I (Kim) remember when I was head of talent

and chief diversity officer at Hasbro in the mid-1990s discussing Workforce 2020. It was a big idea that the workforce would be tremendously different. But for most, it was a concept too far from their reality to address. Well – we are here now. Over 10,000 baby boomers will turn 65 every day for the next 20 years (Hewitt, 2013) and will leave the workforce. Layer on the impact of the COVID-19 pandemic and the "Great Resignation", where millions of people are voluntarily leaving the workforce. We will feel the effects of these dynamics for years to come. Businesses must pivot and get better results to remain healthy.

10. **Lack of concern or alarm.** There is a lack of acknowledgement regarding the size and seriousness of this issue. In many organizations, we have moved away from (or never started in the first place) systematically identifying and cultivating leaders because we are moving too fast, we are too busy, or senior leaders aren't taking it seriously enough. In the CEO study where Kim conducted interviewing 50+ CEOs on determining leadership potential, more than half concluded that they should be doing more to focus on this issue based on the reflections that occurred through the questions asked. There is no better time than now because of the much-discussed war for talent (in other words, the tremendous difficulty in finding and retaining top talent), especially high-potential talent, that derails organizations (Prager et al., 2018).

Definitions and Fundamental Concepts

Before going any further, we should define our terminology.

Leadership. It is the act of galvanizing people, individually and collectively, to achieve profound results that would have otherwise been difficult to achieve independently. It includes creating a vision, providing clarity, and facilitating an effective environment, all for the purpose of enabling employees or a team to be their best selves. The CEO of Aternity, Bill Hewitt, summed up this important concept and put it in context with this quote, "There is no scenario where the manager is successful, and the team fails." By definition, leaders need followers.

Leadership Blueprint (LB). This conceptual framework drives much of our thinking about the factors to consider when determining leadership potential. While we will go into more depth on this framework in a later chapter, it is helpful for you to get an early understanding of the components now. The framework, developed by Church and Silzer (2014), has three dimensions.

- The Foundational Dimension focuses on intelligence and personality.
- The Growth Dimension focuses on learning agility and motivation.
- The Career Dimension concentrates on leadership skills and technical expertise.

The premise is that each dimension serves as a threshold. For example, if the person does not have the necessary cognitive skills or has major personality issues, you likely should not advance the conversation on them about leadership potential.

It is important to note that determining leadership potential should be part of a larger approach to talent management, including recruiting, developing, managing, and retaining top talent. An integrated approach to talent management is the goal (Janson, 2015).

High-potential leaders. For our purposes, high-potential leaders are individuals who demonstrate the strength of intelligence, have no significant derailing personality traits, have high learning agility and high motivation, and have the desire to be a future leader at higher levels in the organization. These individuals often demonstrate high performance in their areas of responsibility. This is not a condition of potential, but a significant factor of importance to many senior leaders.

High performers. These are individuals that may or may not meet the criteria in the LB but are critical to the organizations for the level of work they produce and their high performance. These individuals may or may not be high potentials. Organizations would be well served to identify and reward these employees.

Leadership development. Leadership development is strategically creating the capacity for an organization to perform in the future while simultaneously targeting specific improvement areas in individuals for certain skills or knowledge areas. Developing leaders should include using tools and assessments to help people understand their various strengths, weaknesses, and capabilities. Leadership development comes in many forms, such as new experiences, mentoring, books and articles, and programs.

Leaders vs. managers. There is often great debate about the differences between leadership and management. Simply put, managers are focused on near-term task completion achieved through people. Leadership has a longer-term horizon and typically involves elements like transformation, strategy, and higher levels of business performance. We do not find the distinction critical, at least for this conversation regarding leadership potential. Both leaders and managers have responsibility to people or, said differently, are people with people management responsibilities, so our current conversation applies to both managers and leaders.

Our Definition of Determining Leadership Potential

Determining leadership potential (DLP) is the process, better enabled when using tools and assessments, designed to identify vital characteristics, ideally earlier in a candidate's career, which indicate the likelihood of a candidate possessing the necessary components to be successful as a future leader. It is a key component to an overall talent management approach for an organization. This process uses performance as the ticket to entry into the conversation about whether someone is of high potential, but the person's intelligence, personality, motivational level, and learning agility are the true indicators of potential.

This is a future-focused effort of identifying people who have the capabilities to be successful leaders in the future as indicated by this CEO comment, "people who may not be great leaders now but have the innate characteristics, ability, and the work ethic to challenge themselves and put in the time can develop into a leader." A common pitfall is to use depth in leadership skills as a yardstick (ex. strategic planning, delegation, managing, etc.). These are not good indicators of potential, and we shouldn't be worried if someone doesn't have them because leadership skills are teachable. High potentials early in their career will likely not have these capabilities, but rather need the raw ingredients of intelligence, motivation, personality, and learning agility (IMPL) that we should be looking for to be considered high potential.

A client of Kim's, Terry Considine, CEO of Air Communities and Aimco, has a great way to describe this work when he described looking for acorns that will grow into great and powerful oak trees.

Another client of Kim's was a chairman of a few companies. He had an expression that resonated well. "It takes rock stars and roadies to run a great concert." You need them both to be the best in their role, but the roles are unique and different and require different components. The point here is not everyone needs to be or can be a leader. The other point is that positional/functional players are incredibly important to run the organization. We shouldn't try to make a roadie into a rock star if they don't have the raw ingredients needed, but we should have the best darn roadies around, continue to invest in their skills, and reward them well for doing excellent roadie work. None of that is suggesting we put them in a leadership role because they have been with us for a long time or because they are a great roadie – big difference.

Impact of Poor Leadership

Why is all of this important? The negative impact of poor leadership can have tremendous consequences and, frankly, is unnecessary. It can create an unwanted legacy in an organization for years to come. Poor leadership is costly, diminishes performance, and drives out talent. The list of ineffective leadership behaviors is extensive. Some leaders are disrespectful towards others, act aloof towards employees, are not trustworthy, exhibit negative attitudes, or lack interpersonal skills. Others refuse to hold themselves accountable, act unprofessionally, have poor delegation skills, are absent, lazy, lack the ability to adapt, are inept at decision-making, do not understand the job assigned to them, or cannot compete in changing markets. This does not even include the list of folks who simply lack the cognitive skills to lead their organization through complex problems or dynamic market conditions.

Selecting the wrong person as a leader has significant financial costs – both in terms of hard dollars and intangible impacts. Some researchers estimate the price of a failed leader to be $500,000, while others indicate that the range should be $1.5 to $2.7 million for each leader when factoring in hidden costs (Buckner & Marberry, 2018). Intangible costs include missed opportunities resulting from following a sub-par leader, who may not be driven to achieve the same business results a high-potential leader would be (Gaddis & Foster, 2015). As Alison Croke, CEO, Wood River Health Services and a participant in our CEO study phrased it, "The consequences of [doing a poor job] are felt for quite a while."

Absenteeism is another hidden cost. Employees associated with a leader they do not like, or whom they do not want to work with/for, often have higher absenteeism rates. Several research studies quite tellingly indicated that 70% of workers in the USA would take less pay to be rid of their managers (Hogan et al., 2018). This is a cost to the business because employees who do not come to work cannot (or rather, do not) produce.

Many people are often conflict-avoidant and would instead leave a job rather than have a challenging conversation with or about their manager. It is generally understood that people leave managers, not companies. Turnover is another hard cost as it includes both recruiting time, recruiting fees, the time needed to train a new employee, and the impact of damaging morale when other employees have more work because of vacant roles. Turnover also creates missed opportunities and loss of potential revenue. Poor employee engagement is also an unintended consequence cost as less engaged employees translate into lost productivity. The company misses out on the productivity of that individual and any additional discretionary effort present when employees are highly engaged.

Great Leadership is a Difference Maker

Conversely, great leadership can have an incredibly positive impact. Employees seek to be inspired, respected, and rewarded. When this is done well, powerfully positive leadership can even go so far as significantly increasing shareholder value. A demonstrable correlation exists between selecting and developing the right types of leaders and their eventual effectiveness as leaders.

And it is contagious! Having high-potential leaders in an organization has a positive, cascading impact on many other areas of that organization, beyond simply creating and operationalizing strategy. High-potential leaders are considered more pleasant to work with, more interpersonally attractive, and they improve the retention rate of other employees.

A strong pipeline makes all the difference to an organization. The benefits are clear, but the process required for identifying needed high potentials is robust. Having a clear, defined, and well-understood process with built-in accountability not only has the benefit of producing future leaders but also drives reliable business results.

Here are some examples of that last point. Talented individuals from a high-potential pool are viewed as harder-working employees and stronger problem-solvers (Parr et al., 2016). High-potential leaders see the value of talent and are 84% more likely than their peers to strongly focus their efforts on developing talent (Campbell & Smith, 2010). High-potential leaders create levels of employee engagement that are three times higher than that of their peers, an outcome leading to stronger business results (Sinar & Wellins, 2017). The value of having high-potential people in your organization cannot be overemphasized. Once you have them, you need to keep them. The good news is that, given a robust and effective process of identification of high potentials in an organization, retention rates are increased for existing high potentials (Brant et al., 2008). Winners want to be around winners!

Boards of Directors and CEOs are increasingly turning their attention to these matters. To be the best, a company must have the best, which includes talented leadership ability. While that is obvious, the research truly supports this notion. Companies extending their efforts to identify and develop high-potential employees into leaders will outperform peers (Craig, 2015). One company found that when this work is done well, they outperform the financial results of their peers more than two times (Sinar & Wellins, 2017). Another study showed that organizational outperformance could be upwards of 4.2 times that of their peers when organizations have strong leaders (DDI, 2018).

Think about that statement.

...organizational outperformance could be upwards of 4.2 times that of their peers when organizations have strong leaders.

That's so compelling.

What CEO or board in their right mind would defy such results? The answer seems to be too many – considering the number of organizations that do not do this work well or effectively, as demonstrated by the number of poor leaders in responsible positions. The time is now to change this losing strategy.

Levi Strauss & Co's CEO, Chip Bergh, stated it best during our CEO study interview: "One of the greatest responsibilities of leaders is to identify 'rock stars' and put them on a rock star trajectory, making sure they get the assignments and opportunities they need to meet their full potential."

Organization of this Book

This book is designed to help you be better at determining leadership potential. The chapters are organized into three sections. The first section focuses on foundational ideas. The second section is a deep dive into the elements of the Leadership Blueprint. The last section of this book is focused on how to apply knowledge gained to real-world scenarios.

Foundational Ideas

Chapters 2 through 5 equip you with the foundational knowledge needed to capture our way of thinking in this space.

- Chapter 2 deals with the issue of bias in this work
- Chapter 3 is a deep dive into the Leadership Blueprint
- Chapter 4 examines two of the three leadership studies we conducted on this topic.
- Chapter 5 explores the third study, interviewing 50+ CEOs worldwide. This study had such profound results, and we dedicated an entire chapter to these insights.

Leadership Blueprint

- This section focuses on the foundational dimensions of *intelligence* (cognitive skills) in Chapter 6 and *personality* in Chapter 7.
- The section continues by focusing on the growth dimensions with an emphasis on *motivation* in Chapter 8 and *learning agility* in Chapter 9.

Putting Ideas into Action

- Chapter 10 is dedicated to the concept of tools and assessments to provide you with resources on how to be more data-informed in your efforts to determine leadership potential.
- Chapter 11 rounds out the Leadership Blueprint by concentrating on leadership skills and technical expertise. It includes specific guidance on where to go from here and wraps up the conversation with a summary of final thoughts.

We intend for this book to be helpful to leaders and managers (people with people management responsibilities) at all levels who want to become more proficient at determining leadership potential. We have heard from numerous CEOs that it would benefit CEOs to help guide the talent efforts in their organizations. The book also aims to increase the knowledge base for HR or talent practitioners and professionals. We wrote it to also assist academic professionals in their teachings.

Remember – we have created many resources, including self-assessments and case studies, to assist in your skill development. Those can be found at **determiningleadershippotential.com**.

Summary and Recommended Steps Forward

Consider this chapter and book a call to action. Many people in life have few chances to do grand things that result in creating significant change in the world. However, most of us have everyday chances to make small changes that can make a difference. Placing those who have the greatest potential in leadership roles is one of them.

Let's fix it. The majority of leadership development work to date has been addressing items later in the development process. We have a problem because we haven't truly committed ourselves to fixing the root causes of determining leadership potential…we just try to fix it through leadership development efforts.

How to solve the problem? Don't create the problem in the first place.

Are you truly serious? If so, take these actions:

1. Pick a framework on how to think about DLP and stick to it. We recommend you adopt the Leadership Blueprint – the rest of the book will make the case for it.
2. Develop an intolerance for variation on how the people around you think about DLP. Everyone must use the same lens, use the same framework, use the same language, believe similar things, and understand items in the same way for us to align, and through alignment we will be successful.
3. Commit yourself to become an expert on determining the potential in people. This book is a good start. Read everything you can, practice well, talk about it, and learn from mistakes.

4. Be alarmed. Demonstrate urgency and demand it of others on this issue.
5. Own it. Be the standard-bearer for everyone else on how to determine potential.
6. Read the book and follow the advice in each section.

Visit **determiningleadershippotential.com** for case studies and additional resources.

Reference List

Brant, J., Dooley, R., & Iman, S. (2008). Leadership succession: An approach to filling the pipeline, *Strategic HR Review*, 7(4), 17–24.

Buckner, M., & Marberry, M. (2018). How to identify and grow high potentials: A CEO's perspective with proven results. *People & Strategy*, 41(1), 22–28.

Campbell, M., & Smith, R. (2010). High-potential talent: A view from inside the leadership pipeline. Greensboro, NC: Center for Creative Leadership. www.ccl.org/wp-content/uploads/2016/09/high-potential-talent-center-for-creative-leadership.pdf

Church, A. H. (2015). The pursuit of potential: Six things you need to know about defining potential in your organization. *Talent Quarterly*, 6, 29–35.

Church, A. H., & Silzer, R. (2014). Going behind the corporate curtain with a blueprint for leadership potential. *People & Strategy*, 36(4), 50–58.

Craig, M. (2015). Cost effectiveness of retaining top internal talent in contrast to recruiting top talent. Competition Forum, 13(2), 203–209.

DDI (2018). Five best practices for identifying potential leaders. www.oracle.com/us/products/applications/talent-mgmt-potenital-leaders-2095829.pdf

Gaddis, B. H., & Foster, J. L. (2015). Meta-analysis of dark side personality characteristics and critical work behaviors among leaders across the globe: Findings and implications for leadership development and executive coaching. *Applied Psychology*, 64(1), 25–54.

Hewitt, A. O. N. (2013). *Building the right high potential pool: How organizations define, assess, and calibrate their critical talent.* Aon Hewitt. www.aon.com/attachments/human-capital-consulting/2013_Building_the_Right_High_Potential_Pool_white_paper.pdf

Hieker, C., & Pringle, J. (2021). Leadership development: A $366 billion business. In *The Future of Leadership Development* (pp. 27–48). Palgrave Macmillan, Cham.

Hogan, R., Lusk, D., & Chamorro-Premuzic, T. (2018). Are your HiPos overrated? *People & Strategy, 41*(1), 38–42.

Ignatieva, I., & Babina, E. (2019). Impact of leadership potential on change potential. *Modern Science, 5*, 19–30.

Janson, K. (2015). Demystifying talent management and people development. *Employment Relations Today, 42*(2), 29–35.

Janson, K. M. (2020). *How does assessment of leadership potential differ between organizational levels?* (28025024). Available from Dissertations & Theses @ Northcentral University (2425571024). www.proquest.com/dissertations-theses/how-does-assessment-leadership-potential-differ/docview/2425571024/se-2

Parr, A. D., Lanza, S. T., & Bernthal, P. (2016). Personality profiles of effective leadership performance in assessment centers. *Human Performance, 29*(2), 143–157.

Prager, R. Y., Church, A. H., Silzer, R., & Scott, J. (2018). Getting the best from your high potential leadership: Spotlight on the 2018 leading edge consortium. *TIP: The Industrial-Organizational Psychologist, 56*(2), 63–67.

Sinar, E., & Wellins, R. (2017, July 7). Realizing the potential of high potential pools. DDI. https://web.archive.org/web/20170811235636/www.ddiworld.com/leadership-practices/realizing-the-potential-of-high-potential-pools

Zenger, J., & Folkman, J. (2018). Getting the right people in the Hi-Po pool. *People & Strategy, 41*(1), 28–32.

2

Bias and Determining Leadership Potential

Kimberly Janson, Melody Rawlings and Dani Monroe

This chapter provides insight into the impact of bias on determining leadership potential from a macro perspective. The reality is everyone has biases. Hard stop. It's a reality of being human. These biases continuously inform our judgement of the world and the people around us. We sort people in many ways, such as height, education, car ownership, etc. We put people into social categories based on our beliefs and feelings, which often impacts our ability to determine leadership potential accurately. We will explore some common examples of bias and then identify ways to manage this to determine leadership potential more accurately.

This chapter was important for me (Kim) to write based on my career-long commitment to diversity. I began this journey when I was working for the Bank of Boston and committed myself to help enable a workplace where people had the best chance of success. I volunteered to be part of the very progressive diversity work at the bank at that time. Those of us who volunteered had the opportunity to participate in some immersion training for a few weeks, and frankly, I found it life-changing. This work continued to Hasbro and Heinz. The tagline I created for the work there was D@H = p3...Diversity at Hasbro equals people, products, and profitability. If you get the people piece right...having an environment where people can pull their chairs all the way up to the table and contribute to their fullest, the research says the better products come out of the heterogeneous groups. If you do that, profitability will follow. That's why diversity work is important and why I stand behind it in organizations. It's not altruism or being philanthropic. It's about valuing people and helping them get the most out of themselves because the business prospers when you do.

DOI: 10.4324/9781003272212-2

One of the simplest but most powerful resources I took from the Bank of Boston experience was something called the Assumptions Model. The premise is that we have elements of who we are and experiences in our lives that shape our view of the world. They can be primary elements of influence such as gender or secondary elements of influence such as education, ones we have some choice over.

Think of it this way. Envision the old coffee makers we used in which we placed a paper filter in the coffee machine, placed the coffee in the filter, added water, and voila! Coffee! Now envision that same setup, but the filter is laced with raspberry or chocolate. It influences the coffee. That's what happens to all of us. Some of my filters – being the youngest of ten children, being married, a mom, an equestrian, an academic, an executive, a redhead, etc. – absolutely shape how I view the world. I often remind myself that "the only one having the Kim Janson experience is Kim Janson."

The reality is that we all have filters that, often unconsciously, influence the data we receive. We all do this. We go through life sorting based on our experiences, preferences, effects of conditioning, etc. This sorting includes positive and negative views of people. The downside of biases is when we make incorrect assumptions and then consequently take action that harms others. When we do this as it relates to this subject matter, we may miss people with leadership potential. Therefore, the challenge is it's too easy for us to be biased. We slip and slide right into assumptions. We need to work exponentially more comprehensively and consciously to make sure we periodically examine and actively manage our biases.

Special Note

The work Kim did at the Bank of Boston, referenced above, was led by an *amazing* woman – **Dani Monroe**. She was simply so powerful in her ability to connect with people and help folks see other views of the world. Dani had a profound impact on me and my development. She helped shape my thinking about people, business, diversity, and inclusion before I was even 25 years old. I later went to Hasbro, Inc. (a truly fantastic organization) and created the learning, leadership development, and organizational effectiveness functions. After standing up those functions, I was asked to head up diversity. The first person I called was Dani. I am so proud of the work we did there together. If you research Hasbro, its commitment to diversity and inclusion is evident. I am so delighted with that fact and where they stand today. It started with a tremendous foundation we built together. Even their recognition as a Fortune's Best Company to Work For was started by our diversity work. I remember the very day I introduced the concept to the Board and our intention of pursuing that recognition. The work was so strong that we won the Society for Human Resource Management (SHRM) Innovative Practice Award for our effort and results. Because of that history, I asked Dani to co-author this chapter. She was an obvious choice to help better understand this important topic.

The Science of Bias

For more than 50 years, scientists have been researching the phenomenon that our brains are much better at recognizing faces of our own race than other races. This phenomenon intensifies over time because our brain builds a preference for them (Eberhardt, 2019). This is true, even for babies! From day one, babies start intaking shapes and forms that inform how their brains will transmit data subconsciously. Consequently, our brain also works to categorize our world to make processing information faster and easier. Said differently, our brains are wired to sort things – people, food, ideas, etc. Things, people, and customs that we are familiar with make it much easier to process information and frankly allow us to be able to operate in this world. Unfamiliar situations or lack of exposure to people different than us requires the brain to work harder at assessing differences. Can you imagine if our brains required us to examine each and every piece of information and decide about it? We would all have been eaten by the wooly mammoths and giant sloths a long time ago if this was the case. This sorting and bias processing allows us to safely exist – but it limits us at the same time.

Once we form these categories or frameworks regarding how we think about things, they are tough to change. There is even a dynamic called confirmation bias that works against us in this regard. We, often unconsciously, look to find information that confirms what we think because we trust what we believe even if we are presented with irrefutable information. As a result, through mechanisms such as confirmation bias, our brains enable us to perpetuate and spread ideas that are simply not objectively or factually accurate or make decisions that benefit one group over another.

Bias can sneak into talent management. Consider the last time you were interviewing a person for a significant role, and the applicant happened to be from your college alma mater. You likely felt drawn to this person. You understand how they were trained. Did you use a rigorous questioning process? Not likely. Unconsciously, you were likely practicing confirmation bias.

The consequences of this practice are significant. It means we will operate on little, old, or no new information. It means that we will rely on stereotypes when they support something we perceive to be true or what we are familiar with. Sometimes the association between a group and an idea becomes so strong that we act without thinking about the reality of the given situation in front of us. This is often referred to as implicit bias. Implicit bias is a big idea as it relates to determining leadership potential, so we ask that you stay engaged with this concept a bit further.

Implicit Bias

In 1995, social psychology researchers Anthony Greenwald, PhD, and Mahzarin Banaji, PhD, asserted that the idea of implicit and explicit memory can influence our actions, attitudes, and behaviors. This thinking led Harvard University to its, now widely recognized, tremendous work in implicit bias. Harvard broke down the concept by focusing on the two words. The implicit part is about us being unaware or taking something subjective as absolute. Bias Harvard refers to as essentially being non-neutral or, conversely, having a preference. Even when we are not conscious of it (via the implicit in implicit bias), bias has consequences that we need to understand and mitigate. The stereotypical association we carry in our heads can affect what we perceive, how we think, and our actions. Harvard has even created several tests to help people understand where their implicit biases lie. The Implicit

Association Test has been taken around the world and has 13 categories to assess a person's bias. It helps all of us understand that bias is inherent to our life experiences. Insight such as this can help us understand to where we gravitate, often at a speedy and unconscious level. It puts more consciousness in our choices and decision-making, essential to excelling at determining leadership potential.

In addition to Harvard, there are other reputable thought leaders in this space. For example, the Perception Institute focuses on creating solutions to challenges of race, gender, and other identities. They have emphasized, in their work, how important it is for us to operate at an unconscious level. If you see a crosswalk sign and red light, you stop. You don't think about stopping; you just *do it*. If you were to examine every action such as this, we simply wouldn't be able to function in this complex world. Consequently, so many of our actions occur without consciously thinking about them. The Perception Institute also has strong work in helping us understand the impact of our biases.

Implicit bias also increases the imposter phenomenon (Visram, 2020). The imposter phenomenon or imposter syndrome, which is how it is also known, is reoccurring and extreme self-doubt that causes feelings of not being good enough or the self-perception of being a fraud. A sense of belonging is one of the strongest factors any leader needs to be successful. Women and diverse people suffer from imposter syndrome more often which then compounds the issues of discrimination and implicit bias. The feelings of not being good enough are confirmed by direct or indirect signals that one doesn't belong from the start (Visram, 2020).

Bias and Determining Leadership Potential

McKinsey & Company have conducted several extensive studies regarding the value of diversity and inclusion for a workplace, including examining more than 1000 companies in 15 countries. They began this research in 2014 and have tracked the progress of these companies ever since. According to McKinsey (*Women in the Workplace*, 2021), companies who demonstrate inclusion and value diversity outperform on profitability by 21%. Additionally, the more ethnic and gender representation is present in the senior levels, the wider the gap on profitability between those companies and companies that do not have senior-level women or people of color in their ranks. While this is not a diversity book, it is critical to understand the positive impact that facilitating a diverse and inclusive environment creates, and that consequently makes actively managing our biases become critical.

Before going further, let's define what we mean by equity, diversity, and inclusion. When using the term diversity, the intent is to acknowledge how we are unique and different. Remember the elements that made Kim different in the earlier example – mom, equestrian, executive, redhead, etc. Those are dimensions of diversity. These dimensions are ideological, experiences, physical attributes, etc. Inclusion means that we actively and knowingly recognize and engage in our differences in a significant and intentional way. When we are inclusive, we overtly seek to involve everyone, ensuring the underrepresented are joined up with the rest of the organization to ensure everyone is heard, valued, and has an equal opportunity to contribute, be their best self, and grow.

Equity means that we have built a clear opportunity for everyone to have access to opportunity. That includes hiring, developing people, and promoting people internally. These elements are critical because the diversity of thought, experience, etc., is a true competitive advantage, and it is essential to compete in the global marketplace. Equity and inclusion are central components to ensuring diversity. Therefore, knowing the role bias plays is critical in understanding how to identify high potentials because, if you do not, you may be cutting yourself off from a valuable portion of the talent pipeline or, conversely, blinding yourself to seeing only what you want to see and, in turn, filling the pipeline with people who genuinely do not have the potential. Although often relied upon, merely using intuition and "gut" are not credible strategies for assessing leadership potential (MacRae & Furnham, 2014). Using preference rather than objective data is a concerning tendency based on the dynamics we described in terms of implicit bias (Nolan & Overstreet, 2018).

There are many types of bias in the workplace. Women account for a much smaller percentage of senior leaders, and people of color are also chosen to be leaders at much lower rates (Makino & Oliver, 2019). Gender and racial bias are two obvious and easy-to-track forms of discrimination. There are so many others. Another controversial and straightforward example is a bias against creative people. The same with people who do not work full-time...they also face bias as they may be perceived as less productive, uncommitted, or both.

It is important to address an ongoing comment that is often heard in the context of diversity in organizations. Many people have said, "Yes...but I don't believe in quotas. We need to hire the best person." Our consistent response is – we absolutely need to hire the "best" person we can find for the role. We never should put someone in a role because of their gender or race. It's not good for anyone. However, if we don't set some goals, then it is easy to assume hiring the "best person" is someone who comes from the readily available talent pool. The tough part is that the readily available talent pool is often not a diverse talent pool. It might take more work or more time to identify strong diverse candidates to be part of a robust slate of candidates for a role. Our point here is that it is worthy work to do because hiring a talented *and* diverse workforce has tremendous benefits.

A case in point is part-time faculty in higher education. Melody experienced this at a former institution while teaching as adjunct faculty while completing her doctoral studies. In faculty meetings, full-time faculty were openly given preference for committee work, teaching assignments, and even campus volunteer projects. In one university meeting, a full-time faculty member blatantly stated, "Part-time faculty should have no voice in policy decisions." This wasn't just her experience; it is backed up by studies that reveal the bias against adjunct faculty. Bias comes not only from full-time faculty but also from students as well who have also been shown to be biased against adjunct faculty (Fulk, 2019). This is a simple, non-controversial yet obvious example of bias in play. Certainly, companies and universities can have such policies and practices, but look at how limiting this one is to the development of people who are also teaching their students! These are only a few examples of the many biases that exist. A few others are listed below.

Common Types of Biases at Work: Example – Gender Bias

The first and most sizable example of bias is gender, as there are many examples and much research on this topic. For our purposes, we will speak of cisgender people only. These are people whose personal identity and gender correspond to their assigned male or female gender at birth, and typically this is identification with being either male or female. We are taking this approach as this data has been tracked for a longer period. Research is limited when documenting transgender and nonbinary people or the other six forms of gender. This example illustrates that cisgender bias is consuming and complicated while acknowledging gender identity is fluid. Our intention is to present research that can be extrapolated across all types of gender identities, knowing we are presenting a limited perspective on gender.

Consider these facts that extensive research has illuminated.

Based on identical resumes, men are called to interviews in a higher proportion than women resulting in women being called to interview 30% less often than men (González López et al., 2019). That situation worsens for smart women as men get called back at twice the rate of women when comparing GPAs on their resumes. That number goes to three times the rate when math is the major (Chamorro-Premuzic & Akhtar, 2019). More than 100 countries have laws where it is illegal for women to work certain jobs, according to *The Economist* (May 2018). That doesn't even touch the salary gap that exists. It would take over two hundred years to fix the gap at the current rate of salary growth for women, according to the Wood (2018) of the World Economic Forum. A famous study of orchestra auditions showed women were twice as likely to make it past the first round and three times as likely to make it past the third round if they were blind auditions (Chamorro-Premuzic & Akhtar, 2019). The blind audition acts as a system to mitigate bias. Women were judged simply on how they performed, not how they looked.

A prevalent theme in the research on women as leaders and their potential to assume senior positions is gender bias. There is considerable evidence outlining a clear bias against women in leadership positions. Women are significantly underrepresented in senior roles compared to men in business as well as in academia. Look at these statistics:

- Women typically comprise 20–30% of the vice president and above roles in corporations (*Women in the Workplace*, 2021).
- Women are named CEOs for only 8.2% of the Fortune 500 companies – that's 41 of the 500 companies (Women Business Collaborative, 2021).
- Between entry level and senior level, the number of women of color drops off by 75%, down to 4% (*Women in the Workplace*, 2021).
- Only two black women CEOs are included in the (2021) list of Fortune 500 companies.
- Across the world, women make up only 5% of the CEOs, with men outnumbering women 17 to 1 (Milenkovic, 2021).

- For every 100 men promoted, only 86 women are promoted (*Women in the Workplace*, 2021), creating a smaller pool of female candidates to promote.

COVID-19 has exacerbated this problem with millions of women leaving the workforce. Regardless of specific data indicating that more women have bachelor's degrees, master's degrees, and PhDs (Gipson et al., 2017), women remain underrepresented in senior-level roles. In one study, both men and women considered women to be as capable of being successful in leadership roles as men, yet two-thirds of those surveyed asserted that men would have an easier time achieving those positions (Parker et al., 2020). Men are disproportionately represented when compared to older and female colleagues (Tresh et al., 2019).

Dani Monroe, in *Untapped Talent: Unleashing the Power of the Hidden Workforce* (2013), describes how we have developed a mental model of what makes a good leader. When you think about what a janitor should look like or a professor, these are mental models, and they largely stay fixed in our minds. These models are constructed by our life experiences but also are effects of conditioning by things such as school, family, and, very importantly, the media.

When one drums up the mental model of a leader, it often focuses on traits long considered to be masculine. It often aligns with white males over six feet...you know, people who look like "heroes" in movies or athletes. Consider this...less than 15% of the US population are white men over six feet, but in Fortune 500 companies, that number is 58%. It gets more egregious as men get taller. The percentage of white men 6 feet 2 inches or taller in the US population is 3.9%, yet 30% of Fortune 500 CEOs are (Kaul & Bureau, 2011).

A major contributing factor that enables this dynamic is stereotypes regarding behaviors. Companies hire for "agentic" or male-type behaviors. Yet, when women are evaluated against these behaviors, they are criticized for demonstrating the same behaviors. "Agentic" characteristics include confidence and assertiveness (Gibson et al., 2017). Comparatively, the characteristics often associated with women are lower intelligence, submissiveness, weakness, and more communal traits (Makino & Oliver, 2019). This tendency to lean on agentic characteristics is even more true for roles in a male-dominated industry (Chamorro-Premuzic & Akhtar, 2019). Sadly, one such example is given by Zara

(2018), highlighting a study of when people were asked to name a female tech leader, 8% named Siri or Alexa, and the rest could not name any.

The phrase "think manager – think male" is associated with the belief that leadership and male behavior are synonymous (Chamorro-Premuzic & Akhtar, 2019). The problem is, when women demonstrate behaviors that would be considered managerial quality in a man, some people in organizations reject them because they are violating the behavioral expectations of women and even violating female gender norms (Player et al., 2019). Women are encouraged to adopt "agentic" behaviors but mollify them, so they do not seem strange to men (Gipson et al., 2017) or to other women as well. The process of identifying women leaders is clearly not working well.

This dysfunction is well documented despite the data indicating that women are strong leaders. It is mind-blowing that this is occurring despite the data indicating that companies run by women often have better ROA, ROE, and higher sales.

Women score higher than men on assessments in all dimensions of leadership, except for vision and strategy (Player et al., 2019). Research by the McKinsey Global Institute estimates that $12 trillion could be added to the world economy by 2025 if we had more women in leadership roles (Valerio, 2018). Additionally, the underrepresentation has a significant impact on overall organizational health, as well as social and cultural issues (Player et al., 2019). Research also shows women are more respected, create more followership, communicate better, empower their people, are better problem-solvers, and are fairer (Chamorro-Premuzic & Akhtar, 2019).

Matters are further complicated for women because they often maintain more responsibility outside of work, where most of the domestic duties fall on their shoulders compared to their male counterparts. A resulting problem, often referred to as the pipeline problem, creates a dynamic in which there is a lack of women leaders ready to assume more significant roles. Another topic more often associated with women as compared to men is this idea of culture fit.

Women are not provided with the same amount of feedback as men are nor do they have access to the same level of mentoring (Valerio, 2018). This point is pivotal because mentoring and sponsorship have been determined to be the most impactful development solution – sponsoring even more so than mentoring. Just having younger women in the pipeline will not fix the issue (Valerio, 2018). Women have limited access to developmental opportunities which compounds the lack of pipeline issue, and the problem of underrepresentation severely grows. There is a gendered difference, even when it comes to the types of development that are offered. Women are often offered only remedial development solutions. The double challenge of this incongruence is, when women display these agentic behaviors, they are viewed as unlikeable and do not get hired or promoted (Player et al., 2019). This contributes to women leaving organizations and falling off the high-potential ladder across the board.

One factor that is tricky for women is confidence. Women are viewed as less confident because it is assumed they do not assert themselves in ways such as speaking up or asking for promotions. However, hundreds of studies determined this was not true (Tinsley & Ely, 2018). Compounding this issue is lack of confidence, viewed more negatively for women, and is perceived as a bigger issue for women. Additionally, the perception of women having too much confidence works against women as much as having no confidence but not for men.

It would seem the treatment of women in the workplace is not fact-based but bias-based. We took the time to do a deep dive into gender because, if you look around in your own workplace, evidence is clear of the disproportionate experience women are having as compared to men. Despite the volume of evidence that suggests it should be otherwise, this bias is still happening. Biases are powerful. Implicit biases are dangerous because they are subliminal. We will take you through a few more examples just to provide more context, but the punchline is there is much work to be done in this space, particularly around our own biases.

Dani Monroe shared an observation she made of women leaders in healthcare that attended mixed company meetings. During meetings with men, she said, "women were quiet, did not raise difficult issues and often spoke only when affirming a male's perspective. However, in other meetings where they were the senior leader, the picture was a stark difference. These same women took charge, spoke with confidence, managed the meeting, and didn't hesitate in setting directions." She asked a few women leaders about her observations and the response was less than impressive. "We've learned its best not to make waves, that men have the power in this organization, even though we make up 70 percent of the workforce."

While this is a totally understandable outcome – this idea of not speaking up – unfortunately, it compounds this issue and feeds the implicit biases at play. Much work here to be done...

Common Types of Biases at Work: Example – Racial Bias

So much could be written about racial bias. Not only could this be its own chapter, but it also has been the subject of many, many books. We couldn't possibly do it justice in a brief chapter on determining leadership potential here, but we just wanted to share a few ideas to prompt your thinking because of the enormity of the issue. More work is to be done here, and we strongly encourage you to delve into this area to understand it further.

Race and its impact on diverse people's success are in the DNA of American culture. It may evolve differently around the globe, but the outcomes tend to be the same depending on whether or not diverse people are the majority in a given culture.

- Did you know that black people are less likely to be employed than white people (Quillian et al., 2020)?
- Did you know they have much worse jobs and earn less money than white people even when comparing the same skills and experience?

In a large healthcare organization, the chief diversity officer (CDO) decided to address the myth that diverse candidates were less qualified than their white counterparts. After reviewing a year of applicant data, the CDO discovered that diverse applicants were better qualified than whites but were not hired at the same rate or level within their organization. Data illustrated that diverse candidates held higher-level graduate degrees than their white counterparts while graduating from the same-quality institutions. Bias research has made it clear that bias is a factor in the choices employers make in how diverse people fare in the job search and workplace.

Research economists Marianne Bertrand and Sendhil Mullainathan conducted a famous study in Chicago and Boston where identical fake resumes with one version having black-sounding names and the other version having white-sounding names were sent to 1300 job postings (Bertrand & Mullainathan, 2004). Of the 5000 resumes sent, black-sounding names received 50% fewer calls than white-sounding names regardless of where the ad was placed, or the role advertised. If you can imagine...highly qualified black resumes were called even less (Eberhardt, 2019).

An egregious example of not getting the job was when Nikole Hannah-Jones was denied tenure from the University of North Carolina (UNC). Her application is considered one of the strongest in the school's history and included her being placed in the journalism hall of fame by UNC. Dr. Hannah-Jones is a Pulitzer Prize-winning reporter for the *New York Times* and the founder of the 1619 Project. She was finally offered tenure after a long-protracted fight with the Board. To her credit, she refused UNC's offer and instead accepted the inaugural Knight Chair in Race and Reporting at Howard University to teach students that look like her. She's enjoyed great success since. She received $15 million in an endowment for her work (NAACP Legal Defense and Educational Fund, 2021) and can be seen on all the major news shows.

In another study, researcher Lincoln Quillian, a sociologist, examined 54,000 applications of people applying to 25,000 jobs; whites received 36% more callbacks than blacks and 24% more than Latinos. A meta-analysis of more than two dozen studies examined results from over the last 26 years. It was consistently revealed that blacks and Latinos are disadvantaged by bias in the job search process. As a result, many have taken to anglicizing their names – referred to as whitening the resume – to improve their odds (Eberhardt, 2019).

When a person can't even get in the door, they certainly can't be promoted, but racial bias also shows up in the promotion and advancement of diverse individuals. Mercer Consulting conducts an internal labor market analysis for the organizations each year. Most of their findings demonstrated that diverse talent experiences stagnation at the lower levels of the organization and with very few breakthroughs to the top tier executive level. Take the Latino population, which is about one-fourth of the population of the USA. Yet, only about 4% of Fortune 500 CEOs are Latino (Tapia, 2021). Asians have a similar experience. Asians account for 27% of professionals in the USA, but less than half that number are in leadership roles, and about 1.5% are Fortune 500 corporate officers (Bloomberg, 2020).

If you find this difficult to believe, I invite you to review the demographics in organizations you know. Who sits at the executive, middle manager, and staff levels? In most organizations, those management layers are very homogeneous. Conscious observations of our environments are one of the best tools to mitigate bias.

But, first, you must understand and believe that it exists. Second, we should stop kidding ourselves about the reasons why it exists, so we can begin to do real work around changing it.

Common Types of Biases at Work: Example – Physical Bias

Physical biases exist in many forms, both by attributing more positive feelings towards people with various characteristics and negative emotions towards those who do not. For example, much bias has surfaced against overweight people (Finkelstein et al., 2018). People who are ill also face biases (Carnes et al., 2015), and there are also age biases, with preferences trending toward younger workers fueled by assumptions that older workers have lower levels of productivity (Tresh et al., 2019).

Other physical attributes have influenced whether a person is considered a potential future leader. Remember our statistics about height and CEOs? It does not end there. Research conducted by Effron (2018) shows that taller people earn an extra 1–2% more income for every inch they stand above average. In fact, in America, a person who is six feet tall can be expected to earn $200,000 more in their career than someone who is five feet four inches tall (Chamorro-Premuzic & Akhtar, 2019). Judge and Cable (2004) conducted a study in which it was revealed that height was equal to intelligence (IQ) as a factor that determines if someone would become a leader, regardless of whether height was necessary for the job.

Attractiveness also factors into this effort. More attractive people make more money than less attractive people because the former are viewed as more intelligent, regardless of any evidence supporting that supposition (Korenman et al., 2019). Get this one: one study showed that companies led by CEOs who had wider faces had higher financial returns than those CEOs who had narrower faces (Wong et al., 2011). Why? Because people with wider faces are considered more powerful.

Isn't this insanity?

Let's examine a common bias – redheads. Some common redhead stereotypes are heartbreakers, cool/aloof, or hot-tempered. Well, the authors of this book are both redheads, and some of those descriptors apply to us, and some do not. That's the point. Taking a rule and applying it to a whole entity will produce false results. As an aside, during class introductions in a college class, a professor told Kim that he hated redheads because two ex-girlfriends had broken his heart. He said Kim was going to have to work very hard to get even a decent grade in his class. Kim's mother had to restrain her father, a father to seven girls (and three boys), from showing up on campus! The audacity and idiocy of this professor are happening all day long in organizations.

For the record, in case you were interested, Kim smoked the professor with excellent deliverables so that he had no choice but to give a good grade. During that entire semester, Kim was so distracted by being angry and "showing him" that she learned little. That class did not get her best work or learning because she was more focused on producing revenge work. Looking back, how foolish and what a waste, but at the time, it was real for Kim. That's the insidious impact bias has.

Melody was also singled out by others, including teachers who would jokingly say on the first day of class, "better watch your temper in here!" Throughout elementary and even high school, kids tauntingly teased through chants of "I'd rather be dead than red on the head!"

Many diverse people will tell you that they must work twice as hard to obtain the same level of success as those in dominant positions because they are constantly fighting against stereotypes. Dr. David Thomas, President of Moorehouse, illustrates this in his book *Breaking Through*. He sheds light on the dynamic that diverse and white people with the same qualifications and life experiences can start off in the same position, but over time the white person begins to advance at a more accelerated rate than the diverse person. The difference in success is support from managers, opportunities for development, and promotion. Working twice as hard is not an exaggerated concept. When a diverse person rises to the top, they typically have "superhero" abilities like well-regarded business leaders such as Ursula Burns, former CEO of Xerox, or Carla Harris, Executive Vice Chairman of Morgan Stanley. Implicit or explicit bias has many tendrils, and most are harmful.

Common Types of Biases at Work: Bias of Self-Assessment

One (hysterical) research study conducted by Freund and Kasten (2012) and examined test scores against self-ratings on intelligence. There was less than a 10% overlap between how people perceived themselves and how their intelligence actually tested. It reminded Kim of a *Business*

Week article she read years ago where the research in the article showed 80% of the managers surveyed felt they were in the top 20% of the leaders out there. That math doesn't work. It is common for people to put more faith and trust in their viewpoints and, thus, have an inflated opinion of themselves even if that view contradicts the evidence (Finkelstein et al., 2018).

Self-awareness is a game-changer. It is becoming more and more central to this concept of leadership. Kim recently wrote an article for *Forbes* on leadership potential and self-awareness because of the interdependencies between the two concepts. Kim also was interviewed for a comprehensive article on the topic by Yahoo! Finance because it is an increasingly critical focal point. We often do not see how others experience us, both on the upside of our strengths, positive attributes, and the downside regarding our deficiencies. Our blind spots influence our behaviors such that hitting the mark becomes a guessing game. We give ourselves great credit for our intent, but it is the impact that people feel and measure us by.

This process is a conflict of interest for high potentials in some cases because the manager is often the vehicle that lets a high-potential person be recognized as such (Finkelstein et al., 2018). Many inputs can influence this sponsorship, including whether a person is liked by the manager (Hogan et al., 2018), and can even be further complicated because sometimes managers use their roles to prevent up-and-coming employees from developing because they are fearful for their own jobs. As managers and leaders responsible for determining leadership potential, it is essential that we recognize that we have bias.

In a recent study, Kim conducted interviews with more than 50 CEOs from around the world on leadership potential. This lack of self-awareness surfaced as one of the biggest challenges in determining leadership potential.

- Anand Sivaraman, CEO, Remidio Innovative Solutions, cited his lack of awareness as a big challenge
- Bill Winters, CEO, Standard Charter Bank, spoke of how leading a global organization across 59 countries has required him to continually build his understanding and appreciation of cultures or styles that might be very different than his own
- Joel Stevenson, CEO, Yesware, was concerned about what he wasn't seeing because of his own personal biases

- Julia Stewart, formerly the Chair and CEO of Dine Brands Global spoke of people's inability to clearly view their individual attributes and flaws. This can create an almost insurmountable obstacle in developing and maximizing their own true leadership potential
- Mary Dillon, CEO, Ulta Beauty, spoke of needing to be humble enough to recognize that she does not have all the answers because of her blind spots
- Priya Amin, CEO, Flexible, was concerned about her own biases and lack of self-awareness
- Sharad Joshi, CEO, Satio Inc., said the biggest challenge in determining leadership potential is keeping your own internal biases in check.

These are CEOs of major organizations worldwide, and when asked what the biggest challenges to this work were, they pointed right back to themselves. That's pretty powerful and something for us to take the lead from as we consider our role in determining leadership potential.

Summary and Recommended Path Forward

We are genetically wired to make assumptions to operate in this world. That's the good news and bad news. The challenge is that we move at such a speed that we don't often stop and examine these assumptions and ask ourselves if they are true for the given situation. When you layer on the impact of our values, the effects of conditioning of many things like parents, school, friends, media, etc., the result is that people are operating on lots of different functioning principles that translate into behavior.

If you are truly serious about becoming more competent in this area, start with these steps:

1. Start with the understanding that we are never going to see the "whole picture" and acknowledge we need assistance in filling in the pieces.
2. Acknowledge that we all have biases and do specific work to understand what those biases are and what role they play in our worldview. There are many good books on this. As a start, find two and read them.
3. Get beyond the obviousness of an issue to fully understand it. Don't just head-nod when hearing it; dig under it to understand it.

4. Immerse yourself in someone else's experience. Understand the "why" of the behavior. Truly seek to understand by walking in their shoes.

5. Put practices in place to solicit input and make it part of how you operate. One question I love at the end of client interactions is, "What can I do more or less of to make things even better next time?" We all have blind spots. We need to actively manage our blind spots.

6. Accept that you will never be done. Our beloved and departed father used to put one blinking light on our Christmas tree to remind us of our imperfections and so we could get comfortable with that idea and not stop working on them. A pretty profound and impactful effect of conditioning from Kim's childhood.

7. Get help. The good news is we are all in this together, so reciprocity can be a galvanizing impetus for us to work on ourselves together. Let's try to be more human and be better together.

8. Take the Harvard Implicit Association Test to enlighten yourself about where some of your own blind spots might be.

Visit **determiningleadershippotential.com** for case studies and additional resources.

Reference List

Bertrand, M., & Mullainathan, S. (2004). Are Emily and Greg more employable than Lakisha and Jamal? A field experiment on labor market discrimination. *American economic review*, 94(4), 991–1013.

Bloomberg (2020, May 27). The leadership representation ceiling for Asian Americans. www.bloomberg.com/company/stories/the-leadership-representation-ceiling-for-asian-americans/

Carnes, A., Houghton, J. D., & Ellison, C. N. (2015). What matters most in leader selection? The role of personality and implicit leadership theories, *Leadership & Organization Development Journal*, 36(4), 360–379. doi:10.1108/LODJ-06-2013-0087

Chamorro-Premuzic, T., & Akhtar, R. (2019, May 17). Should companies use AI to assess job candidates? *Harvard Business Review*, 17. https://hbr.org/2019/05/should-companies-use-ai-to-assess-job-candidates

Eberhardt, J. L. (2019). *Biased: Uncovering the hidden prejudice that shapes what we see, think, and do*. Penguin Books, New York.

Effron, M. (2018). *8 steps to high performance: Focus on what you can change (ignore the rest)*. Harvard Business Review Press, Brighton, MA. https://store.hbr.org/product/8-steps-to-high-performance-focus-on-what-you-can-change-ignore-the-rest/10169

Finkelstein, L. M., Costanza, D. P., & Goodwin, G. F. (2018). Do your high potentials have potential? The impact of individual differences and designation on leader success. *Personnel Psychology, 71*(1), 3–22.

Freund, P. A., & Kasten, N. (2012). How smart do you think you are? A meta-analysis on the validity of self-estimates of cognitive ability. *Psychological Bulletin, 138*(2), 296–321. https://doi.org/10.1037/a0026556

Fulk, A. B. (2019, February 14). Confronting biases against adjunct faculty. *Inside Higher Ed.* www.insidehighered.com/advice/2019/02/14/how-bias-toward-adjuncts-plays-out-among-students-other-faculty-and-administrators

Gipson, A. N., Pfaff, D. L., Mendelsohn, D. B., Catenacci, L. T., & Burke, W. W. (2017). Women and leadership: Selection, development, leadership style, and performance. *The Journal of Applied Behavioral Science, 53*(1), 32–65.

González López, M. J., Cortina Trilla, C., & Rodríguez, J. (2019). The role of gender stereotypes in hiring: A field experiment. *European Sociological Review, 35*(2), 187–204.

Hogan, R., Lusk, D., & Chamorro-Premuzic, T. (2018). Are your HiPos overrated? *People & Strategy, 41*(1), 38–42.

Judge, T. A., & Cable, D. M. (2004). The effect of physical height on workplace success and income: Preliminary test of a theoretical model. *Journal of Applied Psychology, 89*(3), 428–441.

Kaul, V., & Bureau, E. T. (2011, September 30). The necktie syndrome: Why CEOS tend to be significantly taller than the average male. *The Economic Times. https://economictimes.indiatimes.com/the-necktie-syndrome-why-ceos-tend-to-be-significantly-taller-than-the-average-male/articleshow/10178115.cms*

Korenman, L. M., Wetzler, E. L., Carroll, M. H., & Velilla, E. V. (2019). Is it in your face?: Exploring the effects of sexual dimorphism on perception of leadership potential. *Military Psychology, 31*(2), 107–116.

MacRae, I., & Furnham, A. (2014). *High potential: How to spot, manage and develop talented people at work*. Bloomsbury Publishing, New York.

Makino, K., & Oliver, C. (2019). Developing diverse leadership pipelines: A requirement for 21st century success. *OD Practitioner, 51*(1), 4–10.

Milenkovic, M. (2021, September 24). The leadership gap: 20 revealing male vs. female CEO statistics. SmallBizGenius. www.smallbizgenius.net/by-the-numbers/male-vs-female-ceo-statistics/

Monroe, D. (2013). *Untapped talent: Unleashing the power of the hidden workforce.* Palgrave Macmillan, New York.

NAACP Legal Defense and Educational Fund (2021, July 6). Nikole Hannah-Jones issues statement on decision to decline tenure offer at University of North Carolina-Chapel Hill and to accept Knight Chair appointment at Howard University. www.naacpldf.org/press-release/nikole-hannah-jones-issues-statement-on-decision-to-decline-tenure-offer-at-university-of-north-carolina-chapel-hill-and-to-accept-knight-chair-appointment-at-howard-university/

Nolan, Jr, M. S. T., & Overstreet, R. E. (2018). Improving how the Air Force develops high-potential officers. *Air & Space Power Journal, 32*(2), 21–36.

Parker, O., Mui, R., & Titus Jr, V. (2020). Unwelcome Voices: The Gender Bias-Mitigating Potential of Unconventionality. *Strategic Management Journal 41*(4), 738–757.

Player, A., Randsley de Moura, G., Leite, A. C., Abrams, D., & Tresh, F. (2019). Overlooked leadership potential: The preference for leadership potential in job candidates who are men vs. women. *Frontiers in Psychology, 10,* 755.

Quillian, L., Lee, J. J., & Oliver, M. (2020). Evidence from field experiments in hiring shows substantial additional racial discrimination after the callback. *Social Forces, 99*(2), 732–759.

Tapia, A. (2021). The Latino leadership shortage. Korn Ferry. www.kornferry.com/insights/this-week-in-leadership/latino-leadership-shortage-autentico

Tinsley, C. H., & Ely, R. J. (2018). What most people get wrong about men and women: Research shows the sexes aren't so different. *Harvard Business Review, 96*(3), 114–121.

Tresh, F., Steeden, B., Randsley de Moura, G., Leite, A. C., Swift, H. J., & Player, A. (2019). Endorsing and reinforcing gender and age stereotypes: The negative effect on self-rated leadership potential for women and older workers. *Frontiers in Psychology, 10,* 688.

Valerio, A. M. (2018). Wherefore art thou all our women high-potentials? *People Strategy, 41,* 32–37.

Visram, Y. (2020, June 3). When implicit bias amplifies impostor syndrome. *Just.* Ontario Bar Association. www.oba.org/JUST/The-Community/2020/May-2020/When-Implicit-Bias-Amplifies-Imposter-Syndrome

Women Business Collaborative (2021, October 14). 8.2% of Fortune 500 CEOs are women, according to the 2021 Women CEOS in America report. Ascend. www.ascendleadership.org/press-release/10-14-prnewswire

Women in the workplace 2021. (2021, November 2). McKinsey & Company. www.mckinsey.com/featured-insights/diversity-and-inclusion/women-in-the-workplace

Wong, E. M., Ormiston, M. E., & Haselhuhn, M. P. (2011). A face only an investor could love: CEOs' facial structure predicts their firms' financial performance. *Psychological Science, 22*(12), 1478–1483.

Wood, J. (2018). *104 countries have laws that prevent women from working in some jobs.* World Economic Forum.

Zara, C. (2018, March 20). People were asked to name women tech leaders: They said "Alexa" and "Siri". *Fast Company Magazine.* www.fastcompany.com/40547212/people-were-asked-to-name-women-tech-leaders-they-said-alexa-and-siri

3
The Leadership Blueprint Explained

Kimberly Janson and Melody Rawlings

This chapter showcases a simple yet powerful framework that can change everything as it relates to more successfully determining leadership potential. As noted in Chapter 1, two of the top ten reasons why determining leadership potential is an issue is the amount of variation in what people think and use and the lack of a clear and agreed-upon framework. There are so many models and theories! Where would one start to have a comprehensive and effective approach to determining leadership potential? The previous chapters have demonstrated that we are suffering from a leadership crisis and a root cause is the lack of effectiveness in determining leadership potential.

No Single Source of Truth

This subject matter is involved in the ongoing and frankly somewhat chaotic debate. Publications on determining leadership potential only surfaced less than 25 years ago, and since then, opinions and publications have significantly evolved in that time, prompting a deluge of theories and models. For example, some focus on traits, while others concentrate on moving up in organizational levels, while still others emphasize using a level-based approach to address leadership potential (ex. can this person move up one or two levels?).

Many of these models/frameworks/theories, created by academics, are criticized for being out of touch with business reality. Conversely, practitioners are criticized for being out of touch with the science and psychology essential in this work. The net result is a lack of clarity and guidance for practitioners, and ultimately the variation we see in how people determine leadership potential.

DOI: 10.4324/9781003272212-3

Creation of the Leadership Blueprint

Faced with this reality, two practitioners created an alternative in the Leadership Blueprint (LB). The LB was created in 2014 by Allan Church and Rob Silzer. Allan cut his teeth on roles at IBM and PwC before spending 20 years at PepsiCo and is currently the SVP of Global Talent Management. His PhD is in organizational psychology, and he was an adjunct professor at Columbia University. Rob was the President at PDI for many years. He was part of the doctoral faculty at Baruch, City University in New York, and he currently is the managing director of HR Assessments and Development, Inc. His PhD is in industrial/organizational and counseling psychology. These two learned and accomplished individuals combined their superpowers to create an incredibly valuable tool in the Leadership Blueprint.

Kim had several occasions to speak with Allan Church regarding the Leadership Blueprint and the concept of potential. He has done great work building a talent system at PepsiCo. He's not only brilliant, but he is a deep subject matter expert in this area. Kim was able to explore various concepts such as emotional intelligence (EQ) and the desire for people to equate EQ to intelligence in error. We also discussed the technology that his team built to enable the Leadership Blueprint framework and the concept of what it takes to create something that is statistically valid and defendable. These conversations helped reinforce what we have been experiencing for more than 40 years in both the business world and academia as it relates to potential – what a profound honor to speak so extensively with this thought leader who willingly gave of his time and had great enthusiasm for the pursuit of extending the work on potential.

The disparate viewpoints in this space led to the creation of the Blueprint. The Blueprint was created after extensive academic research and a comprehensive literature review. This search and analysis extended to existing practitioner tools. The authors looked at applied psychology and organizational behavior research and used data and frameworks from consulting firms. They used studies that benchmarked top companies who were considered to have high-potential practices. In short, they synthesized over 50 years of theories, research, and practice on the subject of high potentials.

Part of the genius of the Blueprint is that it is applied to all levels in organizations. The importance is that it eliminates the dreaded variation that we discussed in Chapter 1 and ensures a consistent lens. The intent behind the model is to create a consistent set of predictors for potential.

The LB has three major dimensions, with each dimension serving as the gatekeeper for the next dimension. Each dimension contains two components and will be detailed in the subsequent chapters. For now, we have provided an overview of the model to help you understand the macro intent of the framework.

- The Foundational Dimension focuses on intelligence and personality.
- The Growth Dimension focuses on learning agility and motivation.
- The Career Dimension concentrates on leadership skills and technical expertise.

Foundational Dimension

This dimension has at its core, a focus on intelligence and personality as determinants of leadership potential. These two elements are in the primary foundational dimension. If a potential leader is not endowed with both intelligence and personality (or rather the absence of derailing personality traits), it is not worth considering them in relation to the other dimensions. This is mainly because both intelligence and personality are largely fixed characteristics.

Intelligence. What people are born with and what they carry throughout their lives are related to cognitive skills. Think of it as processing power, similar to a computer. People can become more knowledgeable, but not smarter. It is necessary to be intellectually honest with ourselves on this point as we consider the strength of people's intelligence and cognitive skills. As you ascend in organizations, the world only becomes more complex for everyone involved, and therefore, leaders need incredibly strong processing power to manage the complexity of the business.

Personality. A tremendous amount of research on personality, several centuries in fact, converged on the understanding of personality as largely fixed. We give life to the personality we were born with through our behaviors. Behaviors are modifiable. Brushing your hair is a behavior. We can do it faster, slower, less, more, sidewise, etc. We can control our behaviors. The challenge is that the more significant a personality trait is for us, the more pronounced the behavior is and the harder it is to access a wider range of behaviors other than that behavior because those traits are so prevalent. For example, if you are extremely focused on detail, it might be hard for you to see the broader picture of reality. The more we have or don't have of something relating to our personality, the more difficult it is for us to control our behaviors. Short of a major life-changing event, like the death of someone close or a serious medical event, we largely stay close to our core personality.

Many personality types make for good leaders. In the next chapter, we will do a deeper dive into personality characteristics that align with strong leadership. For now, the point is to be careful of extreme behaviors that result in derailing personality traits. There is no room for such things in leadership. For example, we should have self-care and advocate for ourselves, but someone who has an extreme self-focus is likely detrimental to other people. The punchline on personality is that we should know it is largely fixed. Therefore, it is wise to carefully avoid putting talent in leadership roles who have components to their personality that are counter to leadership effectiveness and then trying to "fix" them.

If you are considering a candidate for a leadership role and find major flags in either of these components – intelligence or personality – move away from that candidate. Do not be lulled into thinking you can "change" the reality of these elements. These foundational dimensions do not change easily, if ever, in a person's life (Church, 2015).

Growth Dimension

The second dimension is the Growth Dimension, with the two components being learning agility and motivation. This dimension is an equally important threshold to the Foundational Dimension. If the people you are considering do not have high levels of both learning agility and motivation, you should move away from considering them for leadership positions.

Learning agility. Much has been written recently about learning agility. We have dedicated a later chapter to explore this dimension. Ahead of that, recognize that learning agility is essential to a leader's success. The ability to reinvent yourself, to accumulate and assimilate knowledge and experiences quickly, is central to our survival in this crazy dynamic world in which we live. Someone who wants to maintain a static work world, where things are predictable, has little place in the world of work, never mind as a leader. The trap: we as individuals control learning agility. Leaders can't decide this for us. If someone does not want to utilize agility to respond to change, we can do nothing to influence that.

Motivation. Kim often hears leaders say things like, "He's good in such and such an area…if I could only get him motivated …" Right then and there, the manager may as well give up. It is not up to others to motivate leaders. As leaders, they can be inspired, but the choice of how they show up, and what they show up for, is based on their motivation. People choose their level of motivation. It is the proverbial analogy that you can bring a horse to water, but you cannot make them drink. As the owner of a champion-level show jumping business, Kim asserts that is so true. It is also true you need to hire people with a big engine because they must bring it to the vital role of a leader.

If people do not have these two components in spades turn them away. Do yourself and your organization that favor. On the other hand, if they have the components of the Foundational and Growth Dimensions, you can coach and teach them the rest. The rest is what we find in the last dimension, the Career Dimension.

Career Dimension

The focus of this dimension is leadership and functional expertise. This dimension is the most widely targeted component of the Blueprint with many talent management practitioners putting much time and attention towards this dimension.

Leadership expertise. Leadership is a science. As much time and attention should be spent developing deep expertise in this area as one gives to other functional areas of excellence. The good news: many of the skills needed to be a good leader are learnable. Sample skills are setting expectations including effective communication, coaching, delegating, decision-making, and building a highly effective team. If you have the prior four components of our conceptual framework, the Leadership Blueprint, intelligence, motivation, personality, and learning agility (IMPLs) you can learn these as well. (Remember, the Leadership Blueprint has a third dimension (Career Dimension) that focuses on leadership skills and functional expertise.)

Technical expertise. Technical expertise is learnable if you are skilled in each of the IMPLs. Building technical expertise is often a way for people to get noticed in organizations and be granted opportunities to do more in their careers. Performance and having functional excellence are fine gatekeepers for consideration for future roles, but there is a trap. Past performance is not a predictor of future potential and success unless the work is similar. The problem with people having deep functional expertise is that it often does not translate to great leadership. They are entirely different skills. Just because you are fluent in French on Friday doesn't mean you can speak Mandarin on Monday...just because you received a title change. But that's how we treat the role of a leader. "This person is our best engineer; we want to keep him, we need to promote him, have him manage people, etc." Often, there are characteristics existing in some that are fine for an individual contributor where the impact is minimal. Those same characteristics become problematic and not acceptable in leadership roles. This is a significant root cause for why many people are not good leaders. From the start, we set people up to fail.

Measurement and objectivity. A powerful advantage for using the Leadership Blueprint is in the objectivity it brings to this conversation. It coincides with the increased pressure organizations face in how they measure leadership potential. Additionally, the factors it focuses on are too difficult to fake. There are specific ways to measure and more fully understand intelligence, personality, learning agility, and motivation. In addition to using the Blueprint, it is best to pair that work with an internal framework of key leadership competencies needed to be successful in that company. Ultimately, using a multi-trait, multi-method approach (MTMM) will give you the best results. Potential is a multi-faceted entity and is best addressed when using a reliable set of assessments to help measure all aspects of potential.

What the Blueprint is Not

As much as we have covered what the Leadership Blueprint is, it is also important to cover what is not covered in the Blueprint. The Blueprint does not address a few concepts that get a great deal of focus when discussing leadership potential.

- The Blueprint does not specifically focus on how many levels a person will ultimately be able to "jump."
- It does not focus on the speed of promotion or readiness.
- Performance is not addressed in the model.

Where the Leadership Blueprint is being Used

The LB is being used extensively in part or in whole in many organizations. Some organizations use it as the underlying theoretical engine for their work on potential (Silzer et al., 2016). Others are using components of it. Research conducted by Church (2015) indicated that 75% of companies measure and focus on the two components of the Career Dimension – leadership and functional expertise. Another 56% do work relating to the Growth Dimension – learning agility and motivation. And closely following at 52%, the Foundational Dimension – cognitive and personality – is a heavy focus for many organizations. Companies are using the entire LB as well. Eli Lily and Citibank (Church et al., 2015) use the LB as the foundation of its talent process. They couple the LB with psychometric assessments, meetings, and ongoing discussions to formulate their judgement on people's potential (Church & Silzer, 2014).

PepsiCo. One of the most prolific users is PepsiCo. PepsiCo uses the LB as the foundation of its talent management process and as the backbone of its various leadership development programs. Their multi-tier Leadership Assessment and Development Program (LEAD), launched in 2010, has the LB at its core (Church & Silzer, 2014). The talent solutions at PepsiCo also include the Senior Leader Development Center, which focuses on leadership capabilities, personal characteristics, and domain expertise (Church et al., 2017). They pair the LB with their Leadership Effectiveness Framework (LEF), a future-focused set of behaviors customized for various organizational levels to perpetuate talent development for the organization's long-term success (Silzer et al., 2016). The proof is in the pudding because PepsiCo is renowned for its success as an organization but, more importantly, as a producer of great leaders. Having someone from PepsiCo on your team is a near guarantee of a high performer and high potential.

We've used it extensively. We (the authors) are using it everywhere. In many conversations with senior leaders where we are talking about talent, Kim pulls in the four main components to help sort through the conversation and add objectivity. Every time Kim sits with a CEO or senior leader to discuss talent, this framework is used. Clients are using it now by themselves. It is intuitive and practical. It resonates and it works.

Here are four examples of it in play:

Intelligence. A client CEO and Kim were discussing a C-level leader. The CEO is struggling to understand why he is not getting what he needs and wants from this person. I pointed out that he was high on learning agility and motivation. I discussed that he did not have any derailing personality traits and had several positive ones that contributed to his capacity to build strong leaders. The problem was with his cognitive skills. His thinking skills were a bit muddled, and he did not have a strong ability to think systemically big picture or long-term. This was a consistent pattern with this individual. As much as we liked this individual and however strong he was in those other categories, ultimately, he would not be able to give this CEO what he wanted. The CEO needed someone who could be a thought partner at the more strategic level.

Personality. As a former Chief Diversity Officer, I revel in the purity and innovation that happens when different personalities come to work together. However, some personality traits are simply toxic. More on this will be explored in the personality chapter. Extreme introversion, negativity, and self-focus, for example, do not make for good leaders. Those attributes are likely not to change. Narcissism is another example of a toxic trait. One example of a highly narcissistic leader was a woman who was hired in a client company.

We had several strong candidates who may have been game-changers for the company, but the people hiring for that role did not understand what they needed. The hiring team kept talking about preferring someone who was "bubbly," but this was not what was needed in the role. The CEO thought she was terrific, and the company ended up hiring her. Extreme narcissism does not even begin to describe the new hire's true colors. She was paranoid, controlling, vapid, and caustic. She became a known problem. There were complaints to legal and others about her, but the equally ineffectual, indecisive CEO allowed her to stay. She drove troves of people from the organization because of how mind-blowingly horrific she turned out to be. This is a keen example of how not only the individual should be fired but also the CEO for allowing for the creation of a hostile work environment. Personality counts in significant ways!

Motivation. Working with someone who brings brightness, energy, enthusiasm, and motivation to their work can be worth their weight in gold. One client has a leader on the senior team who brought incredible intelligence, some unique raw skills, and deep subject matter expertise. On paper, this person appeared to be a strong leader, except he was not. He led teams during his tenure, but he was not very good at giving them what they needed because he was lazy. He was not motivated to help people be their best selves. He was a completely hands-off leader, and consequently, his team members struggled greatly. The CEO often said, "He's so good in these other areas but if I could just get him to step up, if I could just get him to do the right things as a leader, just motivate him to...". When you hear those things, it should be game over. People are not motivated by others as motivation largely originates from within. People must bring their own engines. Ultimately, I was successful in helping the CEO understand not only the unchangeability of this dynamic but the negative impact it created for the organization. The former leader was moved into an individual contributor role. Everyone was better for it and happier...including him.

Learning agility. It can be heartbreaking to work with talent who is tremendously capable in one or more dimensions but has a fatal flaw in another. One executive had a brilliant mind by all accounts. He knew the market in ways that others did not. He had a lot of passion for his subject matter and was motivated by it. He was personable one-on-one. But he had a few personality elements that made for some difficult challenges, such as strongly preferring to work alone rather than with a team. Those challenging elements were not so deep that they prevented him from success. However, his low learning agility prevented him from being successful. He would have disagreed with that statement because for the things he was interested in, he had a high capacity to pursue, but he refused to adjust and reinvent himself and how he worked in all other areas. The CEO was strongly discouraged from putting him in a C-level role, but inevitably he did just that. It was as much of a failure as those in the organization expected. He elected to leave, attributing it to the organization rather than himself, which was another big commercial for low learning agility.

We will examine each of these dimensions in detail, but ahead of that, we hope the reader will understand the value in the power and simplicity of the integrated LB.

Summary and Recommended Path Forward

The Leadership Blueprint is a true solution for improving the ability to determine leadership potential. It's so intuitively correct. We are so confident of its effectiveness that we wrapped an entire book around it. Its comprehensive, integrative, yet simple approach is the beauty and the power that make the Blueprint so effective.

Hands down, we need intellectual firepower and capable cognitive skills to solve today's challenges. Who could argue with that? We should be vigilant about insisting on them in our leaders. There is no room for leaders with derailing personality traits. Leaders, by definition, need followers so it's absurd to think that polarizing behaviors in any way would be acceptable. Leadership requires certain foundational traits, and self-motivation is a secret sauce that is simply necessary. Learning agility is purely survival if you want to enjoy any type of success today and certainly in leadership roles. When a person possesses motivation and learning agility, we can teach leadership skills and functional skills.

If you are truly serious, start with these steps:

1. Get to know the Leadership Blueprint in and out, backwards and forwards.
2. Do a time study for 30 days and evaluate leaders in your sphere against IMPLs. Reflect on who has what of the IMPLs? Evaluate those who struggle and truly look at why.
3. Share the Leadership Blueprint with your team and insist they become knowledgeable on the framework.
4. Set a goal to weave the big ideas from the Leadership Blueprint into any conversation about talent or organizational performance.
5. Set a Google alert to inform you about any new writings on the topic or any of the components in the Leadership Blueprint.

Visit **determiningleadershippotential.com** for case studies and additional resources.

Reference List

Church, A. H. (2015). The pursuit of potential: Six things you need to know about defining potential in your organization. *Talent Quarterly, 6*, 29–35.

Church, A.H., Del Giudice, M., & Margulies, A. (2017). All that glitters is not gold: Maximizing the impact of executive assessment and development efforts. *Leadership & Organization Development Journal, 38*(6), 765–779. https://doi.org/10.1108/LODJ-05-2016-0127

Church, A. H., Rotolo, C. T., Ginther, N. M., & Levine, R. (2015). How are top companies designing and managing their high-potential programs? A follow-up talent management benchmark study. *Consulting Psychology Journal: Practice and Research, 67*(1), 17–47.

Church, A. H., & Silzer, R. (2014). Going behind the corporate curtain with a blueprint for leadership potential. *People & Strategy*, *36*(4), 50–58.

Silzer, R., Church, A. H., Rotolo, C. T., & Scott, J. C. (2016). IO practice in action: Solving the leadership potential identification challenge in organizations. *Industrial and Organizational Psychology*, *9*(4), 814–830.

4
What the Research Says

Kimberly Janson and Melody Rawlings

This chapter describes the variation in talent identification, selection, and development among leaders who participated in three studies. Variation is not a friend and should be considered one of the greatest root causes for the lack of a pool of great leaders. Leaders making decisions independently in their own business units, and at their own level, create chaos. Building a pipeline of talent is the goal. Every time a leader has a different set of criteria, it creates joints and offshoots in the pipe such that, as water goes through it, it slows it down or diverts it. It is the same with talent. Consistency is needed in thought and action to build a strong pipeline of talent. Not only do the authors know this to be true from their work, but they also conducted several research studies to dig into this dynamic. This chapter will cover the insights discovered in that first qualitative study and the results of a second, global quantitative study.

First Study Summary

The first study on determining leadership potential was a qualitative case study of the real estate industry. Four leaders were interviewed at each of 10 companies. The leaders were at four different levels within the organization, including the CEO. Kim's complete study can be found in the ProQuest dissertation database. This study was sanctioned by the International Review Board (IRB) at Northcentral University – the governing body on studies involving human subjects. The study consisted of qualitative interviews. The intent of the interviews was to understand the tools and criteria being used to determine leadership potential and to detect any variation that existed.

DOI: 10.4324/9781003272212-4

Second Study Summary

The first study was intriguing. However, it focused on only one industry with fewer participants. So, we set out to do it again with a broader array of participants. Additionally, we wanted to add more science by performing a quantitative study. This second study, like the first, was sanctioned and approved by the International Review Board (IRB). For this study, we pulled a sharpshooter quant genius onto the team. Michelle Withers has been a researcher and statistics professor for years at Brigham Young University (BYU) and Independence University and has her bachelor's and master's degrees in statistics. Michelle not only provided the statistical analysis, but she was a keen mind who helped shape the instrument we used and helped shape the pilot to ensure the instrument was defendable and valid.

We dare not burden you with details of all the statistical testing and evidence regarding the study in this chapter. However, a white paper of this study was created and can be found on determiningleadersh ippotential.com or jansonassociates.com and includes all the statistical testing details for those who want to dig deeper. Just know – after numerous statistical tests, the results were extremely consistent across the all the demographic variables and are considered very generalizable because of the little variation across covariates.

There were five big areas to highlight in both studies beginning with the great variation in defining leadership potential as shown in Table 4.1.

1. There was large variation in how leaders defined leadership potential.

In the second study, an open-ended question prompted survey participants to define leadership potential. Comments were sorted into themes. Most responses described characteristics that good leaders possess, and other responses emphasized demonstrated behaviors. Only 12% specifically addressed potential. That means that only 12% of respondents are thinking about leadership potential in a future-focused way and emphasize core capabilities rather than skills that can be learned. It is also a great commercial about why we are in trouble regarding our leadership crisis!

Table 4.1 How study participants defined leadership potential. Themes and sample responses from participants in qualitative case study of one industry.

Theme	Sample responses
Described traits	"Self-awareness, courage, creativity, being a doer, ethics, ability to influence, etc."
Process – described ways they determine leadership potential	"You figure it out by throwing people into situations, escalating the challenges over their career, and seeing how they do."
Emphasized performance/ competence	"It consists of showing enough competency in what you do and promise in what you do to be considered for additional or new responsibilities."
Didn't define but spoke of how difficult it is to determine leadership potential	"It's super tough to define." and "something amorphous – very hard to determine", "it's a tricky thing" or, concerningly, "not sure I thought about it that much".

This is true of what we see in client organizations. When doing talent-planning work, as Kim sits with leaders reviewing members of their teams as they think about promotability and potential, the lack of understanding on how to think about this properly is rampant. "Well...this person is doing a project manager role, but they don't like people, they aren't good about holding people accountable, and they are often late with deliverables. But I have them here as promotable in one to two years." That is a direct quote from a talent planning session just this week...and is indicative of hundreds of comments made all the time in this work. That is insanity. It's no wonder we don't have the leaders we need!

2. How do people think about their role?

Study participants were asked what they thought their role was in determining leadership potential, and a whopping 70% indicated their role was associated with talent identification and assessment. The two other answers offered most were developing talent and managing performance. That should be joyous news!

Leaders need to enable others in the system to also do a great job in this area in addition to doing great work themselves. This is where consistency and clarity are critical. Variation becomes the enemy. Not one individual mentioned their job was to coach the coaches...meaning mentor leaders in the organizations on how to determine leadership potential and hold them accountable for doing a good job. This is a significant area of weakness in organizations. Coaching the coaches requires different skills and activities. We are barely getting people to coach individual contributors or direct reports! Consider this one of the significant reasons why we have so many poor leaders. Because of the absence of this in organizations, variation is allowed to creep in. The result is people who are placed in leadership roles who simply should not be there.

In the second study, when asked what the respondent's role was in determining leadership potential, there was a cluster of responses. Like the first study which was 70%, the majority (66%) indicated they were responsible for assessing and developing talent. Other top answers were responsible for managing high potentials and the recruitment or placement of high-potential employees.

Think of this phenomenon as similar to decorating. Virtually everyone who has ever bought a throw pillow feels like they are a decorator. The reality is that some people, due to a lack of aesthetic sensitivity and vision, probably should not decorate. You know it...you've seen some questionably furnished homes! Exaggerating a point here knowing you have walked into someone's house and said "wow!" to yourself and it was *not* the good kind of wow. It is the same for being a leader. Not everyone was meant to be one, so competence in choosing leaders and the responsibility around that should have more focus and reverence.

3. What criteria do people use?

One of the main questions of this study was what criteria are being used to determine leadership potential. This is where variation showed up in the most significant way – hundreds of descriptors were provided to this question, and in the first study, six themes emerged, as shown in Table 4.2.

In the second study, there was a very different take on the criteria that were needed, as represented in Table 4.3. The difference between the two studies on this question was the second study provided a dropdown menu of options. If nothing else, this question alone substantiates the level of variation in how people are thinking about leadership potential and the necessary criteria that people need to possess.

Table 4.2 Criteria used by study participants to determine leadership potential. Themes and sample responses from participants in qualitative case study of one industry.

Ranking	Theme	Sample comments
1	Performance	"Relentlessly focused on execution", "a doer", "Here at this company, people who can't do quickly leave." "Must be exceeding or mastering the present job."
2	Management skills	"People have to delegate and empower people." "Need to train staff, to be the coach, need to manage by metrics," etc.
3	Emotional intelligence	"Leadership needs to be more than intelligence. What is more important is their EQ." "EQ is important." "Emotional intelligence is important." "People need emotional intelligence", etc. Several participants identified specific elements of EQ such as self-awareness and empathy.
4	Interpersonal effectiveness	"The ability to get people to follow you", "being able to pull other people forward with you and get to the goal", "having compassion and caring, being a good person", "having some charisma so that people will want to follow them", etc.
5	Historical contributions	Schools attended, sports played, military experience, "Whether they have been in the trenches", etc.
6	Communication skills	"Good listener", "how they speak to someone", "being a good listener", "Is the person communicating in an open and collaborative way? Is it positive and effective communication that is written as well as verbal?", "Do they interact or communicate well with their manager but also the people around them and their team?"

Important to note – nearly half of the study participants referenced EQ!

Table 4.3 Criteria used to define leadership potential. Responses by participants in quantitative global study.

Criteria	Times mentioned (%)
Emotional intelligence	34
Problem-solver/decision-maker	26
Collaborative	22
Communicative	22
Ethical	20
Adaptable	20
Authentic	20
Critical thinking	20
Ethical	18
Three-way tie:	17

- Ethical
- High performing/high achiever
- Strategic

4. How many used intelligence, motivation, personality, and learning agility?

The Leadership Blueprint's conceptual framework emphasizes intelligence, motivation, personality, and learning agility (IMPL). Very few participants mentioned these vital criteria in their answers. However, the story changed in each study when asked about each of these directly. Look at Tables 4.4 and 4.5 below. In the first column of each table is the number of times each of these criteria was identified when asked the open question about criteria used. The second column is the percentage of times people said they actually use these criteria. Note the *huge* discrepancies.

We further asked what people were looking for as it relates to each of the IMPLs. Table 4.6 reflects the criteria identified along with the

Table 4.4 Study 1 – IMPL criteria identified by participants in determining leadership potential IMPL responses from participants in qualitative case study of one industry (Janson, 2020).

	Times identified in original criteria noted (%)	Times identified as a criteria when specifically asked (%)
Intelligence	15	85
Motivation	30	85
Personality	10	95
Learning agility	20	80

Table 4.5 Study 2 – IMPL criteria used to determine leadership potential. Prompted and unprompted responses by participants in quantitative global study.

	Times identified in original criteria noted (%)	Times identified as a criteria when specifically asked (%)
Intelligence	15	73
Motivation	22	86
Personality	4	78
Learning agility	2	87

Results are shocking. When asked directly and specifically about each of the IMPLs, the degree to which these numbers rose to nearly 100% for all four criteria is incredible. This study reinforced the tremendous gap between what people are unconsciously looking for and what they should be looking for, as well as emphasized the tremendous amount of variation on how people are thinking as it relates to determining leadership potential. This is great support for the premise of the Leadership Blueprint.

average weighting leaders give each IMPL in the process of determining leadership potential.

As a side note, we do not agree with the weighting conclusion on personality. We think this is due to a lack of proper understanding of personality, social pressure to not say it is important, and not to

Table 4.6 IMPL criteria identified by leaders with average weighting.

What do you look for?

Intelligence (%)	Personality (%)	Motivation (%)	Learning agility (%)
Critical thinking 70 Strategic 69 EI 66% Curiosity 56 Complexity 55	Specific traits 75 Derailing traits 51 Intense traits 45 Missing traits 35	Proactiveness 82 Persistence 75 Effort 70 Focus 63	Change agility 77 Self-awareness 74 People agility 70 Mental agility 57 Results agility 53
Importance rating: 4.10 out of 5	Importance rating: 3.94 out of 5	Importance rating: 4.2 of 5	Importance rating: 4.97 out of 5

Although emotional intelligence was presented as a choice, it is not a true form of intelligence. People have often associated it with EI, but EI it is actually related to personality.

choose it. We believe people put much more weight on personality than they are saying, but it seems a bit taboo to say so. However, when people talk about chemistry, fit, concern about people being "too intelligent," or important traits such as EI, these are all personality factors. We assert that people do not have a clear understanding about personality.

5. What methods are being used to determine leadership potential?

The most significant source of convergence in the study is how people described the way they determine leadership potential. The top three answers offered were observing, interacting, and thorough interviewing. While observation was the clear leader, it was included in only 15% of the answers. The other point of consistency is related to what occurred within the same companies. While there was still variation, these answers were more consistent from level to level than any other questions. Observation was offered as the top choice by more than 80% of the CEOs. Some suggested the use of assessments as the method of choice to determine leadership potential. Myers–Briggs and Enneagrams were specifically mentioned. Others were frank when they simply said they use their "gut feeling."

In the second study, when asked what tools they use, the five most popular choices identified were:

- How they manage key constituents (40%)
- Face-to-face meetings (32%)
- Observation (29%)
- Current performance (28%)
- Provide new opportunities/give new challenges to test employees (26%).

We've got a BIG PROBLEM.

Observation surfaced many times as the way people assess each of the IMPL components. This is on point with what has been our experience in organizations. Most leadership potential is determined by those decision-makers watching employees in action. The problem is most people are not trained observers. This is where the traps of bias are laid. We've established that most don't know what they should look for, most aren't aware of what sits in their filters creating bias, and now we have established that most people are not trained observers. We have a flawed approach to determining leadership potential indeed. It's no wonder we are having a leadership crisis!

As with the first study, we wanted to explore how much the Leadership Blueprint was used to determine leadership potential. When asked the open question of what criteria people are using, we had many choices. Intelligence, motivation, personality, and learning agility were all options on the list to choose from yet they were selected infrequently. Only 33 respondents put intelligence in their top five choices. Personality was not selected in the top five, with only nine people choosing it in total out of the nearly 600 respondents. However, EI, often associated with personality, was rated the top criterion. Motivation was not in the top five, but it was chosen by 49 people in the study as a critical criterion.

The big takeaways:

- It is not readily apparent to identify intelligence, motivation, personality, and learning agility as criteria, but there is almost universal agreement that they are critical criteria when people are asked directly about them.

- The amount of variation that came when asking people simple questions is staggering.
- In many cases, people are operating without fully understanding what they are doing (ex. personality).

Summary and Recommended Path Forward

Leadership research bifurcates into leadership effectiveness and leadership assessment, with the predominance of research being in leadership effectiveness. We contributed to this thought leadership with two significant studies. The qualitative case study querying many real estate company executives (four at each level) was a great illustration of the variation that exists in what people are looking for at each level to determine leadership potential. This is not a business case for the variation; rather, a default of poor talent management systems. The second study was a global quantitative study in which we applied our hypothesis from the first study. We wanted hard numbers and we got them. For example, when we asked participants what they use as criteria to determine leadership potential vs. asking them specifically whether they use intelligence, motivation, personality, and learning agility...there was, on average, nearly a 70% increase in agreement on each of those four criteria. Something is wrong here. We are missing a critical set of criteria being top of mind for folks when they think about leadership potential. Our research also showed many leaders are not thinking about determining leadership potential at all, and if they are, it is not fleshed out. The other discovery confirmed from these two studies that came to the surface in our scrubbing of *all* the research available was there is no single source of truth when it comes to determining leadership potential.

The other insight to mention is that our fear about performance being used as a criterion was confirmed, especially being the top criterion in our first study. That's so bad! It has such far-reaching implications. Performance is *not* an indicator of potential *unless* the jobs and work are quite similar. This is how we have easily referenced examples of the best technician (ex. accountant, IT professional, designer, etc.) being promoted into a leadership role because they have done great work, but it is a *disaster*. Performance should be only the ticket to entry into the conversation about whether someone has the components of being a high potential.

These research studies also laid the groundwork for the criticality of emotional intelligence and began to help us understand it in the context of personality.

If you are truly serious, start with these steps:

1. Read the dissertation to understand the first study more fully. www.proquest.com/openview/e4c0d7da06bf6aff114784d 376e79389/1.pdf?pq-origsite=gscholar&cbl=18750&diss=y
2. Read the white paper to understand the details more fully for the global, second study which can be found on determiningleadersh ippotential.com
3. Start some experiments in your own circle. Ask how people define leadership potential, what criteria they use, how they think about IMPLs, etc. This will help you understand the conversation and their thinking which will better position you on how to influence their thinking.
4. Identify strong researchers, through LinkedIn or a Google Alert, and stay current with their writings. We certainly hope you stick with us (jansonassociates.com, determiningleadershippotential .com, www.ncu.edu/center-advancement-virtual-organizations) but also Syd Finkelstein, Allan Church, Rob Silzer, Tomas Chamorro-Premuzic, etc. are ones to follow.
5. Develop a well-informed point of view and have an elevator pitch that synthesizes big points into how you speak with others.

Visit **determiningleadershippotential.com** for case studies and additional resources.

Reference List

Janson, K. M. (2020). *How does assessment of leadership potential differ between organizational levels?* (28025024). Available from Dissertations & Theses @ Northcentral University. (2425571024). www.proquest.com/ dissertations-theses/how-does-assessment-leadership-potential-differ/ docview/2425571024/se-2

Janson, K., & Rawlings, M. (2022). *White Paper Determining Leadership Potential Quantitative Study Summary & Recommendations*. www. determiningleadershippotential.com/_files/ugd/b96f80_d400e3ce1c9f49b 58307b027dc0c4125.pdf

5
What CEOs Say

Kimberly Janson and Melody Rawlings

This chapter provides an in-depth discussion of the results from a diverse global study of CEOs and how they determine leadership potential in others and their overall thoughts about leadership potential. Since CEOs are the senior-most people in organizations responsible for organizational focus and priorities, they should take center stage in the conversation on determining leadership potential. Because of their busy lives and the fact that they are fully engrossed in running the business, they often do not have opportunities to provide thought leadership on key areas. The generous CEOs who participated in this study found it critical to be part of this work because of the impact of doing it well *and* not doing it well has on business...and the world. The study included 51 CEOs. A complete list of CEOs can be found in the appendix sections. The participants were global and diverse by gender: 39 from the US and 12 from outside the US; and 12 women and 39 men. CEO biographies and organization demographics can also be found at **determiningleadershippotential.com**. Extensive qualitative and quantitative data analysis was conducted on the 51 hour-long interviews with the CEOs.

An interesting dynamic to note...using a scale of 1 to 5, with 5 being extremely proficient, CEOs rated themselves only a **3.53** on average regarding how effective they viewed themselves as in determining leadership potential. The most successful people who arguably should be the best at determining leadership potential say that they have lots of room to grow in terms of competence in these areas. That should be a giant shove to the rest of us to up our game in this area. Take a moment to let that sink in...

DOI: 10.4324/9781003272212-5

How CEOs Determine Leadership Potential

There were three significant ways in which leadership potential was defined. Those themes were descriptive words, intense words, and interpersonal terms.

Descriptive words. A total of 29 CEOs (56%) used interpersonally descriptive words to answer the question, "How do you define leadership potential?" A sampling of such descriptors includes humility, work ethic, courage, accountability, charisma, initiative, role model, strategic thinker, self-aware, and belief that leadership is a privilege. Sharon Price John – CEO, Build-A-Bear Workshop, Inc.– offered a great example of this.

> You are looking for intellectual curiosity, the ability to visualize initial outcomes and communicate those potential outcomes in a way that people can understand. Clearly, they need a certain level of pure intelligence, but other attributes are also important including vision, some natural competitiveness, and drive to win. However, that winning attitude does not need to be negative, such as an inability to bring people with you or an "I win, you lose" belief, but in a "when we win, we all win" way. Finally – tenacity and persistence are really key.

Intensity. A related way in which people answered the question of leadership potential was to use descriptive words that suggested a level of intensity, energy, or activity. A sampling of these descriptors was grit, curiosity, growth, driver, competitive, risk-taker, tenacity, and ability to learn. David Page – Chairman, the Swift Group – offered a great example of this type of response.

> Someone may not be a great leader right now but has the innate characteristics, ability, and the work ethic to challenge themselves and put in the time to develop into a leader.

And Patrick McMullan, CEO of Three Square Market, adds:

> I will say this, I don't put people in leadership positions that haven't been in highly competitive situations. Whether it's something in sports, academics, or they were in a job previously where they won an internship contest or something, that's a requirement. If they haven't done that, then I just don't consider that person for leadership roles.

Interpersonal terms. The third theme from about half of the CEOs, was to define leadership potential in terms of interpersonal or humanistic terms. Representative terms included caring, commitment, character, ability to create followership, listening, selflessness, collaboration, trust, communication, emotional intelligence (EI/EQ), empathy, and influence. Niren Chaudhary – CEO, Panera Bread – offered an exceptional answer, with heavy emphasis on interpersonal terms:

> Leadership is not just about competence, which I think is somewhat misunderstood – you have to be good, so you have to have personal credibility. Beyond competence, you need character to build trust. When you have competence and character, you're able to show up as trustworthy, consistent, and thereby able to build trust. Once you build trust with the people that you lead, you're able to then inspire them to achieve incredible things.

Chip Bergh, CEO of Levi Strauss & Co, agreed with his statement:

> Character is the biggest thing.

Priya Amin, CEO of Flexible, used two powerful terms in her answer:

> Humble and vulnerable.

Some other interesting definitions offered by our CEOs were the following. Referencing an internal framework his company uses:

> Need to have a combination of the SIZZLE. It's a document we created that defines who and what we are. It declares what we expect from our people, and it also declares what they can expect from us.
> Michael O'Donnell, Chairman, Ruth's Hospitality
> Group, Inc.

> I think someone who has demonstrated a capacity to take ambiguity and create clarity. I think someone who has been able to problem-solve. I think someone who has failed and been resilient and demonstrated an ability to recover. And someone, ultimately, who connects with people in a way that fosters community and fosters performance. That would be the beginning of my definition.
> Victor Velazquez, Executive Director (CEO),
> Maryland State Bar Association

> Potential makes me pause and think because potential is something that's unleashed. It exists, but maybe it's not implemented or executed. Potential makes me think more about leadership and makes me think of words like firing and invoking competence, modeling the proper behavior, and driving for success.
> Siobhan Dullea, CEO of MassChallenge

Our Recommended Definition

Determining leadership potential is the process designed to identify vital characteristics in talent that indicate one's likelihood of possessing the necessary components to be a future successful leader. The process should use tools and assessments to help complement and validate observations. The critical criteria should be intelligence, personality, motivation, and learning agility. The earlier this assessment and determination is done in a person's career, the better they can focus and maximize development opportunities.

How CEOs View Their Role in DLP

When CEOs were asked what they viewed their role to be in determining leadership potential for their organizations, several key themes emerged.

Assist. The first theme was to assist those who have less experience. This could consist of leading by example, encouraging employees, challenging them, or helping them execute their plans. Jane Page, CEO of Lionstone Investments:

> My job is to grow leaders and put out a strategic plan for others to follow. It's my job to help my team lead and do their job, but it's not my job to do their job. That's what I determine as my role as CEO. I give input, collaborate with people, and give direction for the firm while also helping everyone execute their plans.

Organizational structure. Another theme that surfaced related to the need to ensure structure around this work. Representative comments included setting a vision, ensuring people have the right tools, hiring people who align to the mission, etc. Tim Kilpin, CEO of PlayMonster:

> I'm continually assessing. First of all, I'm challenging myself on a kind of regular basis. I'm a big believer in talent management processes, especially for larger companies. Frankly, it doesn't matter what size company; you still have to do it. You have to have a conversation about, "Do I have the right people in the right roles and how do I assess that? Are they setting goals for themselves? Am I able to manage and evaluate their performance against those goals? Am I thinking about succession planning? Am I thinking

about how they've structured their organizations or their teams? Am I challenging them regularly to step further out, to think more broadly? Are they doing those things I just suggested I think they need to be doing as leaders?" I'm always doing that.

Process. A third theme, indicated by 28 CEOs, focused on the process components of this work, such as identifying, observing, assessing, and deciding whether people are high potential. Brian Cornell, CEO, Target:

> I think determining leadership potential is the most important role I play at Target. I have to focus on strategy and some of our business's day-to-day operations and hold responsibility from an external standpoint to work with investors and stakeholders. And as a CEO of a large company like Target, I've got to be focused each and every day on the company purpose and company culture, ensuring we have a pipeline of talent within the organization. I had a board meeting just yesterday; we always talk about talent, leadership, and potential people who are in the pipeline to do more. We spent a lot of time on succession. I personally spend time with different groups within our organization; for example, spending even more time with our Black officers and leaders. My job is to assess the talent and decide where the high potentials are that we can continue to groom and develop to do more. As a CEO today, I think that one of your top priorities is identifying leadership talent, identifying the high potentials, and making sure we're taking the time to continue to accelerate and develop their leadership skills.

Encouraging. A fourth theme indicated CEOs encouraging high-potential employees in some way. Representative comments included empowering people, bringing out the best in others, working together, getting to know the talent, building them up, etc.

Frank Roe – CEO, SmartBear Software – expressed it this way:

> I would say my role is to empower and get the most out of everyone. A key to this is to make sure that there's a platform and a culture here that embraced change, accountability, empowerment and promotions. Simply, I've benefited from being promoted. By working hard, I was given the opportunity to be promoted and not have to jump companies to get that type of promotion. This is the kind of environment that I've tried hard to emphasize and create here. We're in a fortunate circumstance where we've doubled the company in three years, and we're on a path to doubling it again. This expansion affords opportunities for growth, and that growth, in turn, can come either from outside the company or from internal promotions.

Norman Soutar, CEO, William Jackson Food Group, shared another way to be encouraging by breaking down hierarchical barriers:

> Having shared language and facilitating a learning culture where people are encouraged to learn and develop new skills. I also think it helps to not be too hierarchal. As a leader, I think it is important to be visible to all the businesses and know people at all company levels. Being personable with everybody is important.

Developing talent. A final theme that emerged was leaders recognizing their responsibility to do less and develop more. Ken Hicks, CEO, Academy Sports + Outdoors, tells this great story of when he learned this lesson early in life during his service for the military:

> Well, I was fortunate because I went to a school that's mission was to train leaders...I was the best gunner person to shoot cannons in my unit...I realized that my job was not to shoot a cannon as the commander...I could only fire one gun at a time and the Battery would therefore only be 18% effective if I was the gunner...To be a hundred percent effective, I needed to develop people who could train their people to do the job better than I could do it...That was probably my first lesson of understanding that a leader's job is to develop and train other leaders and not necessarily to do.

John Miller, CEO, Denny's, shares this quote about his role of being an enabler:

> I tend to be better at bringing out the best in others, which I've discovered and refined over the years. I've also learned not to be ashamed or embarrassed about saying what I do out loud. We often will have this humility about what we do as you don't want to be obnoxious, but at the same time, that's really what I'm good at. I'm not good at anything else. I tend to mine people's unique capabilities and how they fit together to make a powerful team. So that's what I focus on.

Christelle Colman, CEO, Elite Risk Acceptances, shared his view on his role with this comment:

> I look at every person I employ as someone who's able to walk the journey with us over the next 5 or 10 or 15 years. I'm very aware of the fact that the team is expanding and expanding and expanding all the time, so I need people who can scale their leadership abilities. I've always been extremely focused on female leadership. I've been on the receiving end of criticism over the years that I've just kept my head down. Whenever I have an opportunity to employ individuals, I do tend to look at a female leader.

This comment by Vineet Kumar, CEO, Intellyk, Inc., is one that many leaders and employees wish their CEO would embrace because we often have leaders operating one or two levels below where they should be in the organization.

> I consider the biggest part of my role is growing next level of lead-ers or finding the leaders in every level of the organization. And I'll tell you, the reason for it is not something that I learned 10 or 20 years ago. I've been in the business for now 22 years. I didn't have that insight, probably, five years ago. But I have gone through so many years of my own, succeeding and failing in various things that I've done. When I wake up, I look at what can I do that the rest of the company, or the people in the company are not going to be able to do? I should not be doing things that someone else can do.

How CEOs Learned about Their DLP Role

Experience. The most significant responses pertained to CEOs learning of this responsibility based on their mistakes and experiences they had that helped them acknowledge or understand the criticality of doing this work and doing it well. Slightly more men than women, percent-age-wise, answered the question in this way, with 61% of the overall group offering such explanations. Representative comments included:

- "Trial and error. Making mistakes, realizing what worked, what didn't work when I was not doing well," Samir Patel, CEO, Moonlight Therapeutics, Inc.
- "Observe. What's working and what's not, then make decisions accordingly," Frank Roe, CEO, SmartBear Software
- "Maturity. I've been a CEO since I was 27 years old and have worked at different-sized companies ranging anywhere from startups to 1000-person firms," David Page, Chairman of the Swift Group
- "Learned all along the way," Kevin Chaplin, CEO, SA Ubuntu Foundation & Amy Foundation.

An additional comment from Kevin Chaplin, CEO, SA Ubuntu Foundation & Amy Foundation, illustrates the intentionality that some leaders have about their role and passing their lessons along to others:

> I think it's just a tapestry or the journey that my life took that con-veyed my role in determining leadership potential. In my book, I share about all the lessons, stories, and messages that I learned throughout

my life that I want to use as tools for others to become leaders…I saw all the mistakes they made and by some people who had high IQ and low EQ. I just learned all along the way. I watched other people, I learned from other people, and I implemented. That's what I think got me to the point what I realized what I need to do as a leader.

Role models. Another large grouping (29 CEOs) was those learning from role models who did this work well. CEOs described this in terms of both people they wanted to emulate and those they observed and never wanted to be like.

Below is a sampling of the many wonderful examples.

- Bill Hewitt, CEO, Aternity, spoke of observing his father, who was an IBM executive, practice servant leadership.
- Jane Page, CEO, Lionstone Investments, spoke of watching her mom, who had her EdD in psychology and was a business consultant.
- John Miller, CEO, Denny's, spoke of his mentor Bill Wall, the creator of Taco Bueno; and Norman Brinker, CEO, Chili's, referenced a world-renowned physicist, Richard Feynman, as a respected thought leader he followed.
- Alessandro Felici spoke of his prior CEO, Stefano Clini, and HR Head, Valentino D'Antonio, who shaped him greatly.
- I was tremendously humbled when David Page, Chairman, the Swift Group, referenced a great mentor who opened his eyes, and it turned out to be me (Kim)! A proud moment, indeed.

Tom O'Mara, CEO, Eligius Advisory, LLC, had a different set of people who had a profound impact on him:

So how did they learn that? I think it was from observation. What I saw was a young guy working on Wall Street at the time. I was like, wait a second, some of these people…I want to be like that guy because he is successful, or that woman is successful because of the things they do. Not necessarily because of their title, I think that's what I thought I wanted to be, one of the best in the room, not necessarily the boss in the room, if that makes sense.

Reading/programs. Another smaller theme included learning through books and articles (10 CEOs).

- "I read history and management books. I follow the GE stuff, read *Harvard Business Review*, and all those types of things," John Lawlor, CEO, Maugel Architects.

- An additional minor theme (14% of CEOs total) indicated they learned it through strong leadership training programs or good HR practices.
  - "I had the good fortune of spending about 20 years of my career working for PepsiCo, a great global company...a company that certainly invested in talent development, holds people to very high standards and is willing to invest and give people various opportunities," Brian Cornell, CEO, Target.
  - "I spent 20 years at P&G. P&G has a reputation for being a talent engine," Chip Bergh, CEO, Levi Strauss & Co.
  - "I used to go to Executive Focus International (EFI) conferences in Florida," John Lawlor, CEO, Maugel Architects.

I must say my favorite quote came from Sharon Price John, CEO, Build-A-Bear Workshop, Inc. The program she references, I (Kim) built from scratch from a previous collaboration with Vijay Govindarajan, Syd Finkelstein, Marshall Goldsmith, Kevin Lane Keller, and others. I conceived of it, built it, and garnered great support for it. Hearing Sharon speak so fondly of it, and that it became a big catalyst for her to be the terrific CEO she is today, is profoundly gratifying.

> An important learning moment occurred for me at Hasbro during an executive offsite at Dartmouth. Marshall Goldsmith was speaking, and I was fortunate enough to have lunch with him. He had recently written the book *What Got You Here Won't Get You There*. The conversation highlighted a classic problem from the book where you are so sure of a certain skill that has served you well, that you don't always realize it could be the same tendency that is holding you back. In fact, because this skill has likely been part of what you attribute to your success, sometimes it is the last thing you want to change. His guidance helped me to an "aha" moment, that if I didn't evolve, I may never get to the next level. It can take a lot of bravery to let go of certain skills you have worked so hard to master, but sometimes it is the only path forward.
>
> Sharon Price John – CEO, Build-A-Bear Workshop, Inc.

Self-discovery

Lastly, a smaller group of participants (10) indicated it is part of who they are and knew it throughout their lives. There were several examples of how this occurred. The one offered by Julia Stewart, CEO, Alurx, indicated how much she had to learn it by herself:

I have often been asked about my own leadership capability. I have had plenty of time to reflect and realize the true answer is a blended one. I have had a rich and fruitful career from which I gleaned wisdom from watching and learning from many executives. I wish more of those executives had been female mentors. But sadly, for far too long there has been a dearth of female leaders in corporate America. I also realized I have an inherent natural curiosity which I harnessed to motivate and push myself throughout my career.

CEO Criteria for DLP

CEOs provided a plethora of answers to the question regarding what criteria they use to determine leadership potential shown. The most common response by far was the ability to create followership. Considering our prior global quantitative study as a reference point, we compared both studies' top answers and frequencies. The Global Study on Determining Leadership Potential (GDLP) stands for the quantitative International Review Board-sanctioned survey. The GDLP was open to a wide array of people, including leaders at all levels and CEOs in organizations, whereas the CEO study only included CEOs. Table 5.1 reflects how CEOs in the study ranked the criteria they use to determine leadership potential.

Figure 5.1 reflects the increases that occurred when comparing the results when CEOs were asked specifically about each IMPL.

Ranking? CEOs were asked to weigh each IMPL in terms of how much weight each carried in their decision-making. When compared to each other, they were close in importance and value, but there were definite leaders. The results indicated *learning agility* is slightly more important than *motivation*. Closely following and tied for third were *intelligence* and *personality*.

The following sections are a summary of the specific questions asked about each IMPL, including, do you use this as a criterion? and how do you assess each of these criteria?

Intelligence

When asked, 49 of the 51 CEOs in the study stated they do indeed use intelligence as a criterion of leadership potential. Most wholeheartedly agreed with the critical importance of intelligence. When speaking of

Table 5.1 Ranking of criteria to determine leadership potential. Responses by CEOs in the Global Study on Determining Leadership Potential.

Top GDLP criteria	Frequency %	Top CEO criteria	Frequency %
1. Emotional intelligence	7.06	Followership	8.16
2. Problem-solver/ decision-maker	5.41	Curiosity	4.59
3. Communicative	4.59	Performance	4.08
4. Adaptable	4.12	Empathetic	3.57
5. Authentic	4.12	Communicate	3.57
6. Critical thinker	4.12	Long term	3.06
7. Ethical	3.87	Integrity/honest	3.06
8. Strategic	3.66	Humble	3.06
9. Collaborative	3.61	Good listener	3.06
10. High-performing/ high-achieving	3.61	Collaborative	3.06

intelligence, the following themes emerged as part of the comments they offered.

- **Minimum threshold.** When answering this question, some indicated they used intelligence as a minimum threshold to continue the evaluation process.
- **Components.** Descriptions included how they interpreted and absorbed information, the strength of their analytical skills, evaluated situations and made decisions, their ability to connect the dots, their ability to control their thinking, and their ability to explain complex topics in simple terms.
- **Social intelligence.** Some CEOs spoke of person-centered qualities (e.g., intuition, creativity) and social interaction, specifically indicating their emotional intelligence as a component.
- **Methods.** There were an array of ways in which these CEOs determine intelligence. Some examined what they studied; others looked at the quality of work and outcomes. Many (14 CEOs) used tests.

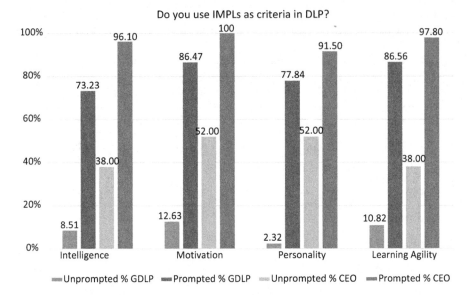

Figure 5.1 Comparison of prompted and unprompted responses in GDLP and CEO studies about using IMPLs as criteria. Figure created by authors.

Still others, 13, spoke of observing people and, specifically, watching how they interact (15), while others spoke of various skills such as thinking in the future or thinking on their feet. Several mentioned behaviors such as vocal speed, vocabulary usage, and funnily enough…humor.

- **Role-specific.** Some indicated it is important but more for some roles vs. others.
- **Too intelligent?** One of the most interesting results was the number of CEOs (8) who spoke about intelligence by expressing concern about potential leaders being too intelligent. Additionally, several CEOs wanted to distinguish book-smart from street-smart and emphasized street-smart.

Personality

All but two CEOs indicated that personality was important. Several themes emerged when CEOs were discussing personality.

- **It's important.** Many CEOs straight-up agreed and emphasized the importance of personality when determining leadership potential.

- **Diversity.** Another set of CEOs (13) emphasized that many personality types will satisfactorily work in leadership, and that diversity is important.
- **What to look for.** When speaking about personality in the interviews, many CEOs indicated what they look for related to personality, such as collaboration, willingness to change, someone who is engaging, social capabilities, humor, niceness, trustworthiness, etc.
- **Humility** was a theme for five CEOs.
- **Hogan.** Many descriptors aligned with various scales on the Hogan Assessment.
- **What not to look for.** Ten CEOs spoke about the concern of derailing attributes such as condescension, obnoxious, rude, negative, pointed fingers, etc.
- **Chemistry is critical.** Thirteen CEOs specifically identified chemistry as a critical factor when discussing personality. Through this portion of the interviews, it was interesting how much CEOs did not want to emphasize personality, but rather other elements such as chemistry, emotional intelligence, etc., when in reality, these are just different ways to suggest personality.
- **Emotional intelligence.** EI was the most prominent topic raised by CEOs, mentioned specifically by 18 CEOs.
- **Empathy.** An additional 11 leaders spoke of empathy. Emotional intelligence is largely defined as having the four components of self-awareness, self-regulation, trust, and empathy.
- **How to assess.** When asked how people consider personality, a variety of answers were given. Examples included a "walk-through" of the resume, asking about challenges that happened in people's lives, about hobbies, achievements, interests, etc. Some wanted to hear how they talked about such things, and to assess whether there was an element of negativity. Other CEOs spoke of observing folks as they interact with them, and another CEO offered the strategy to examine people's social media strategy to see how they engage the world.
- **Assessments.** Assessments were a common topic.

Mary Dillon – CEO of Ulta Beauty – provided an extremely powerful quote relating to personality.

> There's not a personality type I'm looking for. There's a type of chemistry I'm looking for. I don't care if somebody is introverted or extroverted or what their interests are in life. I care that they can collaborate with us, respect other people's opinions, and have the emotional intelligence to know how to work with their peers to get a better solution.

Motivation

The quantitative analysis indicates that motivation is necessary when it comes to DLP. Every participant stated they used motivation in the process and had an average importance level of 4 out of 5. The following themes emerged through CEO discussions on motivation.

- **Yes!** Much of the CEO's discussions reinforced the notion that motivation was critical.
- **What it looks like.** A variety of elements were offered in terms of what motivation looks like. Descriptors included initiative, energy level, intentionality, the ability to create followership, the intent to make the most of life, the most of themselves, the most of the others, entrepreneurial, self-starters, etc.
- **Intrinsic motivation.** Seven CEOs spoke about the importance of people being intrinsically motivated. A prevailing thought provided was the concept of external motivators running their course.
- **How to detect it.** Sources included the interview process, observing, asking open-ended questions that often had nothing to do with work, when people come with ideas, or seek more. Resiliency and examining the candidate's background were also mentioned.
- **Ambition.** Nine CEOs raised the concept of ambition in relation to motivation. Seven CEOs expressed that too much ambition can be as troublesome as not enough.

Learning Agility

Learning agility was ranked second out of the four IMPLs in terms of importance. The following categories reflect the large variety of ways in which CEOs discussed learning agility. The following categories reflect the large variety of ways in which CEOs discussed learning agility.

- **Curiosity.** The most common association of learning agility, detected through the comments of ten CEOs, was to link learning agility to curiosity.
- **Adaptability.** The second most common way (9 CEOs) in which CEOs spoke of learning agility was in the realm of needing to be adaptive to be able to "keep up" and stay relevant.
- **Every day.** Seven CEOs emphasized the need to grow every day in their reflections on learning agility. For example, being hungry to

learn, continuing to learn every day, having the drive to want to learn every day, being proactive and learning on the go, changing direction, constantly learning, and moving, and recognizing that learning never stops.

- **Intelligence and motivation.** Nine CEOs indicated that they associated two other IMPLs – learning agility with motivation or intelligence.
- **Job-specific.** Some CEOs indicated that learning agility was more important earlier in a career because there is so much to learn. Others indicated it becomes more important the more senior you are in a role based on the roles' increasing complexity.
- **Consequence of not learning.** Five CEOs specifically spoke of the consequence of not having strong learning agility. They reflected on whether people are "ahead of the curve or behind the curve."
- **How to assess.** Several methods were being employed to assess leadership potential, as indicated by the CEOs' responses to this question. Three CEOs mentioned using tools such as assessments, case studies, or tests. Most of the other reactions are related to observation in one form or another.
- **Observing.** Many CEOs spoke of observing learning agility. There were several elements these CEOs were observing. One such element was proficiency and competence in articulation and use of language. Other CEOs indicated they assessed this through questioning in the interview process; some examined the use of storytelling. Other modes of observing included how they applied knowledge they had learned and what they did with it. Several CEOs noted that it is the observation of work performed, such as assessing their work through projects. Other CEOs mentioned seeking whether others take risks and observe if they are curious, do they problem-solve, and how do they collaborate. Several CEOs indicated they use demonstrated curiosity as a method to assess learning agility.

Clayton Adams – CEO, Mascoma Savings Bank – provided a sound summary quote about the understated treatment of learning agility, and the importance people place on it.

> Yes, we do. Not formally, but I think that it is definitely a criterion that will be inherent in those who are more successful.

The results of this study should also remind us that we need to be much more disciplined about determining the leadership potential in others. To assist with that, the next four chapters take a deep dive into each of the dimensions of the Leadership Blueprint. In these following few chapters, we will more fully outline what each dimension looks like, make strong suggestions on how to assess it, identify the pitfalls typically experienced and clear up any points of confusion about each dimension. We are well on our way to changing the lens we use in determining leadership potential, and it is long overdue. In the immortal words of the great (and Kim's beloved) quarterback Tom Brady...*"Let's gooooooo!!"*

Summary and Recommended Path Forward

What a tremendous honor and privilege it was to spend time with these successful and influential people in the CEO study. The willingness to give of themselves for the betterment of others to learn from them – the good and the bad – was not only appreciated but admirable. The outputs in this study were mixed. The sage advice and perspective were powerful, and yet the variation we saw in the prior studies existed in this population as well. Said differently, they are not immune to the elements holding us back from more effectiveness in determining leadership potential.

This crew gave us lots of color on personality in particular. They were almost unilateral in their perspective that a big portion of their role is in talent assessment and identification. An interesting insight is that the experience of the interview acted as a mirror for many of these CEOs, giving them the opportunity to reflect on practices, in terms of how much they are thinking (or rather not thinking) about DLP and how much of a gap there is in their organizations as a result. Some left the interviews with a clear commitment to engage with their senior team based on the reflection they did in the interviews. Much of the commentary surrounded this idea that building leaders is the long game, starting of course with the right people. It is through intentionality over time with the *right* profile of people that you can build a stable of strong leaders.

Use the CEO offerings as a comprehensive list of thought joggers to aid your work in determining leadership potential:

1. Get the full results of the study by visiting determiningleadershippo tential.com
2. Identify a few of the top CEOs and follow their success and their writings. Ken Hicks at Academy Sports + Outdoors, Dick Johnson at Foot Locker, Brian Cornell at Target, Niren Chaudhary at Panera, Jane Page at Lionstone, Mary Dillon at Ulta Beauty, Mike O'Donnell

at Ruth's Hospitality Group, Inc., Julia Stewart at Alurx, from so many great companies, and so many more...amazing thought leaders. Be a student and continue to watch and listen.

3. Reach out to your own senior leaders and ask them similar questions to the ones that were asked in the CEO study.
4. Share the insights of this study widely. Highlight and bring their quotes with you. Think robustly about what they offered and bring it into conversations and share tidbits about what struck you from the offerings of various leaders.
5. Make a list of the best ideas they suggest and begin incorporating them in a steady and fulsome way.

Visit **determiningleadershippotential.com** for case studies and additional resources.

6
What do We Mean by Intelligence?

Kimberly Janson and Melody Rawlings

In previous chapters, a case was made for why intelligence is a critical component when assessing leadership potential. Recall, intelligence is fixed, meaning what we are born with is what we have in terms of raw intellectual capacity. Knowledge is different. Knowledge is information, skills, or facts we obtain through a learning event such as education or experience. Knowledge is acquired over time through several mediums, of which "books" might be one. We can and should accumulate knowledge our whole life. Knowledge is increasable while intelligence is not. This chapter describes the importance of using intelligence as a criterion because business problems, work, and life become more complex as you ascend leadership roles. Figure 6.1 depicts the wide agreement in both studies about the importance of intelligence.

Once people focused on it, the value placed on intelligence was clear. It is concerning that it is not front of mind when CEOs are asked what criteria they use, which can lead to variation or not spending time appropriately assessing intelligence.

With the wide agreement on its importance, here are some illustrative quotes from the CEO study on this topic:

- "The role of that test is not to have someone get high marks but to actually break them and see how they think as they struggle on questions." – Matt Barrie, Chief Executive, Freelancer.com
- "Not talking just about IQ but an understanding of complex issues and nuances, not seeing everything as black and white." – Alison Croke, CEO, Wood River Health Services

DOI: 10.4324/9781003272212-6

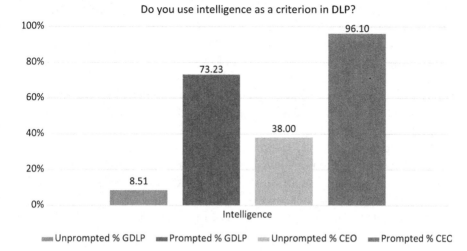

Figure 6.1 How CEOs use intelligence as a DLP criterion. Comparison of responses to DLP criterion when prompted versus unprompted. Figure created by authors.

- "Leadership at the highest level gets trickier and tricker. Will they go off the rails? It doesn't take much to negatively impact a brand or company." – Chip Bergh, CEO, Levi Strauss & Co.
- "The ability to conceptualize for me is number one." – Mark Cutifani, CEO, Anglo American
- "You can be incredibly intelligent and not have a desire. I think it's table stakes, meaning it's not 50% of what I'm deciding, it's 100% of what I'm deciding that I am going to spend my time on. I only have so much time." – Michael Levy, CEO, Crow Holdings
- "It starts with being very intelligent." – Niël Pretorius, CEO, DRDGold Limited
- "You have to be bright, and you have to be quick-bright. I find that the greatest characteristic that those people have is an insatiable curiosity about how things work. The people that I found who have that trait and are really bright have the ability to understand." – Mike O'Donnell, Chairman, Ruth's Hospitality Group Inc.
- "I define aptitude as critical thinking, the intellect, and the ability to grasp new models and frameworks for that sort of business acumen and credibility." – Siobhan Dullea, CEO, MassChallenge

One element of ongoing conversations is the idea of "potential for what?" This question surfaced as it relates to intelligence because some leaders feel it is important but more so for some specific roles vs. others. A few representative comments are below.

- "I use dimensions of intelligence. I think it depends on the role. I think for certain roles, it's incredibly important." – Alessandro Felici, CEO, Evlonet
- "Intelligence, I think, is critically important and certainly in our more technical areas. As we hire thousands of engineers, we're certainly spending a lot of time understanding their technical skills and abilities." – Brian Cornell, CEO, Target
- "Some roles require a certain level of intellectual aptitude." – Sharad Joshi, CEO, Satio Inc.

The big idea here is context does matter to some degree. Still, when you get into more senior roles, regardless of what the company does, you need to lean on intelligence heavily as a component for assessing potential.

Viewed as a Minimum Threshold

The Leadership Blueprint asserts intelligence is a threshold. If people don't have a strong enough intellectual capacity, it is an immediate limiter of potential. That may seem harsh but look at what happened to organizations during the 2020 pandemic. Many businesses' models changed completely without notice and immediately. While not to this extreme, leaders are faced with needing to pivot their functions or organizations because of shifting customer needs, changing markets, etc., all the time. Some CEOs in our study indicated they also use intelligence as a minimum threshold to continue in the evaluation process when answering this question. Representative comments include:

- "It's a screen-out in a sense." – Joel Stevenson, CEO, Yesware
- "You need some level of intelligence, but we are not looking for academic geniuses." – Austin Allison, CEO, Pacaso
- "I think it [intelligence] is table stakes, meaning it's not 50% of what I'm deciding, it's 100% of what I'm deciding." – Mike O'Donnell, CEO, Ruth's Hospitality Group, Inc.

- "Intelligence is a 5 as a necessary condition, but then it becomes a 2 or 3." – Bill Winters, CEO, Standard Charter Bank
- "Your intelligence, your actual hard skills, etc., gets you noticed, but it's really learning how to read the room, learning how to identify talent, and learning how to convince people to go in your direction." – John Holmes, CEO, AAR
- "For a senior level executive, there would be a base level expectation of that." – Mary Dillon, CEO, Ulta Beauty
- "You are looking for intellectual curiosity, the ability to visualize initial outcomes and communicate those goals and outcomes in a way people can understand. Clearly, they need a certain level of pure intelligence." – Sharon Price John, CEO, Build-A-Bear Workshop, Inc.
- "In my view, if they don't have the capability, they're not going to get to the higher levels. It's a necessary but not sufficient." – Mark Cutifani, CEO, Anglo American

With the agreement that intelligence is an important determinant of potential, we need to become proficient at identifying people with strong intellectual capabilities. This starts with clarity on what we should be searching for.

What do People Look For?

Even though it is not an actual form of intellectual intelligence, people associate emotional intelligence with intellectual capability, so we included it on the list of offerings for both personality and intelligence. It was initially associated with intellectual capacity, but further research has suggested it demonstrates interpersonal and personal effectiveness, including people's ability to manage interpersonal difficulties. It was included here because of some participants' association with intelligence and our desire to test how people think about it. It was also included in the section we queried on personality, where it belongs.

Several CEOs explained they were looking for a combination of these attributes identified above as it relates to intelligence. What is meant by this is they do not look for intelligence but how it manifests, such as problem-solving, decision-making, etc. Illustrative comments are listed below.

- "We look at an individual's critical thinking ability, the capacity to cull through lots of information and to find the most important pieces, and their ability to put the company first." – John Lawlor, CEO, Maugel Architects
- "People who can figure things out for themselves." – Melissa Hubbard, CEO, Kerrits Activewear, LLC
- "I look at an intelligent person as someone who's able to cut through the chaff and bring it to either a demonstration of the analytical or emotional intelligence through decisions that they would take initiative." – Anand Sivaraman, CEO, Remidio Innovative Solutions
- "I look at their thinking, decision-making, and judgment – is it sound?" – Jyoti Gupta, CEO, Volk Optical
- "It's about problem-solving." – Bill Hewitt, CEO, Aternity
- "I think you want people that have the intellectual capacity to learn, question, and ask things. I think it's more around intellectual curiosity and capacity than it is pure intelligence." – Dick Johnson, CEO, Foot Locker
- "The focus on the thinking." – Kevin Chaplin, CEO, SA Ubuntu Foundation & Amy Foundation
- "The ability to see trends, then connect the dots that are not always linear, that others often do not see, is very valuable. Combining that with the ability to create a vision that is believable and passionately lead people to a desired outcome is really powerful." – Sharon Price John, CEO, Build-A-Bear Workshop, Inc.
- "Conceptual ability, analytical skills, and commercial frameworks." – Niren Chaudhary, CEO, Panera Bread
- "Can they set up the situation and get to the recommendation quickly and succinctly and then back up the recommendation with rationale?" – Chip Bergh, CEO, Levi Strauss & Co
- "How quickly can they comprehend something?" – Robin van Rozen, CEO, Glen Dimplex Consumer Appliances
- "Think in a kind of organized way/plan work in an organized way." – Alessandro Felici, CEO, Evlonet
- "Situational awareness." – Niël Pretorius, CEO, DRDGold Limited
- "When I look for actual intelligence, I look for how people think and rationalize, and problem-solve." – unnamed CEO, biotechnology firm

- "I also look at the intellectual capability, how smart are they? How agile is their thinking? Are they set in their ways or are they open to different ways of thinking? Agile thinking – can they shift their view or opinion when presented with new information." – Jyoti Gupta, CEO, Volk Optical
- "Good decision-making and the ability to weave together divergent points of view and develop the right solution." – Trey Sutten, CEO, Cardinal Innovations Healthcare
- "You can see someone's intelligence through their world view. By seeing how they contextualize and appreciate something. Situational awareness. They 'just get it.' The way they communicate – their interactions, how they converse and process and exchange information." Niël Pretorius, CEO, DRDGold Limited
- "Of course, we do an assessment for people coming into new roles, but for me, you see it in harmony. How quickly can they comprehend something? Can they turn complex ideas into understandable language? How many topics can they understand? So, for me, it's more in the day-to-day operations. That's why I said before, it's important to see people in action. Can they actually handle complex topics and how they handled it? It's more about if you just have a conversation and you see that somebody could comprehend things quickly. I think that's the best indicator of intelligence." Robin van Rozen, CEO, Glen Dimplex Consumer Appliances
- "I would think that you need some intellectual quickness, the ability to take a lot of data and synthesize it and distill. I would also add, and this might be a little bit off the reservation as it were, but I find that someone who doesn't take themselves too seriously, can have a sense of humor, tends to differentiate." – Victor Velazquez, Executive Director (CEO), Maryland State Bar Association

How to Assess It?

The following is a cadre of behavioral indications CEOs provided regarding how they thought about assessing intelligence. It is a good list of thought-jogger ideas on how to look for it in your own folks:

- "Someone is struggling to keep up with the conversation…or not quick on their feet. It takes multiple explanations." – Coco Brown, CEO, The Athena Alliance
- "Situational awareness…" – Julia Stewart, CEO, Alurx

- "You can see in how they respond to questions that they just 'get it.'" – Niël Pretorius, CEO, DRDGold Limited
- "Getting to know their work lets you get to know how their brain works." – Nachi Junankar, CEO, Avrio
- "Through the use of analogies." – Dick Johnson, CEO, Foot Locker
- "Use a professional to help you assess." – Mark Cutifani, CEO, Anglo American
- "Use an external executive coach." – David Hurwitz, CEO, Transaction Capital
- "A witty sense of humor can indicate a different level of intelligence, curiosity and intellectual quickness." – John Holmes, CEO, AAR
- "Can they turn complex ideas into understandable language?" – Robin van Rozen, CEO, Glen Dimplex Consumer Appliances
- "By how they answer three questions – what, so what, now what?" – Jandel T. Allen-Davis, CEO, Craig Hospital
- "The ability to synthesize information is a good indicator of intellectual capacity because you need to process a lot of information in a hurry." – Bill Hewitt, CEO, Aternity
- "Can they build an argument? Can they make something less complex? I can tell by their writing. Can they set a situation and get to the recommendation quickly and succinctly; then back up their recommendation with rationale? Being raised at Procter & Gamble (P&G), I learned how to write the one-page memo. Every word mattered and you had to be disciplined." Chip Bergh, CEO, Levi Strauss & Co.

Too Intelligent?

Surprisingly, one of the most interesting results of our research was the number of CEOs (8) who spoke about intelligence by expressing concern about potential leaders being too intelligent. This was raised in the first study as well. Additionally, several CEOs wanted to distinguish book smart from street smart and placed emphasis on street smart. Book smarts seem to be about knowledge acquisition and potentially cognitive capabilities, whereas street smarts seem to be about cognitive capabilities and maybe experience. Representative comments were:

- "Intelligence can be a blessing and a curse...extremely intelligent people can get lost in the details." – Joel Stevenson, CEO, Yesware
- "The smartest people don't always make the best decisions." – Jane Page, CEO, Lionstone Investments

- "It's necessary, but not sufficient [intelligence] because I've worked with some of the smartest people globally, and it doesn't mean they're particularly successful." – Michael Levy, CEO, Crow Holdings
- "I've had Harvard MBAs who worked for me who ended up being complete washouts when it came to leading a team." – Tim Kilpin, CEO, PlayMonster
- "I think it needs to be practical intelligence, being able to apply intelligence. I've come across many Harvard and Stanford graduates who have no problem letting you know they came from Stanford, and yet they can't tie their shoes." – unnamed CEO, biotechnology firm

Kim's experience is that high-performing organizations and strong CEOs want people with tremendous intellectual capabilities. However, it is often the case that the higher the IQ, the lower the EQ. This is the issue identified in the quotes above. It's not one or the other, it's both that are essential.

Summary and Recommended Path Forward

The case is clear for why we should source for intelligence as part of our work in determining leadership potential. While not readily apparent when asked about criteria they used to DLP, people heartily agreed it is critical, and on average gave it 4.10 out of 5 in terms of weight in their decisions. The CEOs were a great source of insight about the requirement of intelligence and how to think about it, going so far as many of them saying it should be used as a minimum threshold. If you recall, that's a central tenet of the Leadership Blueprint as well.

When asked what intelligence looks like, people identified critical thinking skills, strategic thinking skills, intellectual curiosity, and the ability to generate and manage complex ideas. Many also associated, mistakenly, emotional intelligence with cognitive capabilities. Some pushed back that "these people don't need to be rocket scientists." No, they don't, and many rocket scientists wouldn't be great leaders even if they are outstanding technicians, but these folks should have strong mental processing skills to be able to grow and evolve with their business and teams. The idea of being too intelligent was raised by some, but that is more of a problem with personality. As important as cognitive skills are to the study participants, and in our experience, we found there were very few folks practicing good techniques to accurately determine intelligence. Let's get better at this by bringing more science and data into the conversation.

If you are truly serious, start with these steps:

1. Get clear on what intelligence is and what it looks like so you can be on the hunt for it.
2. Be rigorous and demanding of people. Make them justify their thinking and points of view so you can watch their thought process.
3. Test them. We advocate literally testing them – we like the Wonderlic and some other critical thinking type assessments, but some are doing great things with simulations and even case studies.
4. Be courageous in talent conversations. Put your foot down if someone does not have enough cognitive horsepower. It is often silent when you do this because it is a bit of taboo, but people actually don't disagree in the long run.
5. Introduce this concept into your conversations and be sure to keep helping people separate intelligence from knowledge. We often hear about the need for "street smarts," but in reality, they are talking about analytical skills, working over complex ideas, etc. Look for the underpinning of what people are saying and mean about cognitive horsepower and help educate and evolve people's familiarity with this topic.

Visit **determiningleadershippotential.com** for case studies and additional resources.

7
What do We Mean by Personality?

Kimberly Janson and Melody Rawlings

This chapter delivers an in-depth discussion on personality and how it is used as a reliable predictor of potential. Personality is one of the trickiest and most significant challenges to people's success in the workplace. It's also the most misunderstood. It's the one we fool ourselves about in terms of being able to "change" or develop through coaching. While that may be the case for some behavior change, if traits are deeply rooted in someone's personality, they are extremely difficult to change. We tell our clients – don't hire or promote someone with the caveat that you are going to change something fundamentally in their personality. It's a losing proposition. To use personality to its fullest and to make sure it doesn't become a source of false hope and ultimately leadership ineffectiveness, a thorough understanding of the elements pertaining to personality is required to be able to use it as a competitive advantage rather than the root cause of failure.

Personality is the set of traits/attributes/characteristics that form an individual's identity (Church & Ezama, 2020). It encompasses the different patterns in thinking, feeling, and believing, which are typically similar and consistent for an individual across various situations over an extended period (Le Sante et al., 2021). Personality is largely viewed as fixed except for those who have had major traumatic events in their lives or those who have fully dedicated themselves to grind through the hard work of changing a fundamental characteristic (Church & Ezama, 2020). The vast majority of researchers agree with this sentiment.

Our assertion, along with many researchers, is that it takes tremendous commitment, ownership, deep self-reflection, self-truth, hard work, and grit to change elemental components of our behavior. Our experience is that most people don't do the hard work that is required to

DOI: 10.4324/9781003272212-7

fundamentally change something. Many are not self-aware enough to even understand the issue fully. Organizations and leaders complicate this by being woefully inadequate in helping people truly understand how others are experiencing them. Determining potential is about making an educated guess and betting on someone. Betting on someone changing something so ingrained and so significant in their life is not a good bet to take.

According to the Leadership Blueprint, as we now know, personality is one of four reliable predictors of potential. Personality can help predict the effectiveness of one's ability to manage, get promotions, job performance, and potential for bigger leadership roles. This has been proven through studies for the last 30 years showcasing many leaders who are both skilled and intelligent but failed because they couldn't build a team, build relationships, deal with complex ideas, delegate, or other core personality traits that people were not able to overcome.

To be clear, we are not advocating for any particular personality type. Instead, we will advocate for specific traits that, in our experience and influenced by research, make for a more impactful leader in our last chapter of this book. The big truth is many personality types work well as leaders. Our biggest focus and contribution to the personality conversation in relation to potential is to raise a flag for us to vigilantly watch out for derailing personality traits. As Hogan Assessments would refer to them, we all have dark side traits to our personalities. We will get into this further when we address what the research says on what to avoid.

Wide Agreement about Personality

As practitioners, academic researchers, and deep subject matter experts, we know personality to be a major influence in whether someone will be effective in a leadership role. Countless research supports this assertion, but also *our* research and 40+ years of practical experience in working with leaders support this assertion. It is less about specific personality types and more about avoiding derailing personality traits that derail someone's effectiveness.

As illustrated in Figure 7.1, many CEOs straight-up agreed and emphasized the importance of personality when determining leadership potential. The first bar represents the number of times personality was

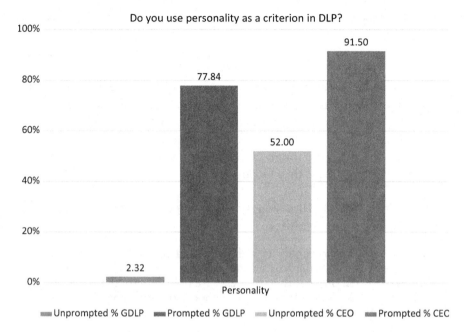

Figure 7.1 How CEOs use personality as a DLP criterion. Figure created by authors.

identified in the GDLP as a criterion to DLP when unprompted. The second bar indicates the percentage of participants in the GDLP who use personality as a criterion when prompted. The third and fourth bars reflect the same information for the CEO study.

Representative comments of a dozen CEOs are:

- "If you have the right personality, many things can be taught." – Melissa Hubbard, CEO, Kerrits Activewear, LLC
- "I think personality can help determine what kind of a leader someone will be." – Jane Page, CEO, Lionstone Investments
- "Personality tells a long story about initiative and ability to handle the different things." – Alessandro Felici, CEO, Evlonet
- "It's really important to me." – Samir Patel, CEO, Moonlight Therapeutics, Inc.
- "As far as individuals that can create followership within their organizations…I think personality does have a lot to do with this." – David Page, Chairman, The Swift Group
- "Of late, I realized my mistake in not giving it its importance because, especially when you're now going to be teams and the

leaders, personality is showing up as extremely important. I used to associate personality with certain defined roles, but now I realized that it needs to be probably more important than I've been giving so far." – Anand Sivaraman, CEO, Remidio Innovative Solutions

- "Do I look at personality traits? Yes. Do I see that people demonstrate them? Yes. Do I think that sometimes those tests can be wrong? Not often. Sooner or later, whatever the test said will manifest itself. Then you get to decide whether that's a risk you want to take. Is it a big enough challenge for you?" – Mike O'Donnell, CEO, Ruth's Hospitality Group Inc.

Mary Dillon – CEO, Ulta Beauty – provided an extremely powerful quote relating to personality.

> There's not a personality type I'm looking for. There's a type of chemistry I'm looking for. I don't care if somebody is introverted or extroverted or what their interests are in life. I care that they can collaborate with us, respect other people's opinions, and have the emotional intelligence to know how to work with their peers to get a better solution.

What do You Look For?

Now, the million-dollar question is, what is it about the personality you should look for in your assessment of folks? This is where it can get wild because there are so many points of view regarding what is important relating to personality. In our global quantitative survey study, we asked people to choose what they looked for. We provided a dropdown menu of choices on that survey. The selected options and the percentage of times they were chosen are below.

- Possess specific traits (74%)
- Derailing personality traits (51%)
- Intensity of traits (45%)
- Absence of traits (35%)
- Other (summary): examples of specific traits they possess

In both the CEO study and the global study, participants were asked to identify the criteria they used. The table reflects the top ten choices that were identified in each study. The difference between the two studies, to keep in mind, is the global survey offered a long list of personality characteristics to choose from, whereas the CEO study asked a broad, open-ended question without any suggestions. In both studies, the top choice in each study only accounted for 7–8% of the total number of traits identified! Once again, the degree of variation is astonishing.

Emotional intelligence is the game-changer. The term emotional intelligence (EI or EQ) has only been around since the early 90s but has grown disproportionately fast in recent years with the onset of research that connects high EI with career success (De Bruin, 2012). Many studies show the trend of people, including CEOs, who are hired for IQ

Table 7.1 Ranking of criteria to determine leadership potential by CEOs in the Global Study on Determining Leadership Potential

Top GDLP criteria	Frequency (%)	Top CEO criteria	Frequency (%)
Emotional intelligence	7.06	Followership	8.16
Problem-solver/decision-maker	5.41	Curiosity	4.59
Communicative	4.59	Performance	4.08
Adaptable	4.12	Empathetic	3.57
Authentic	4.12	Communicative	3.57
Critical thinker	4.12	Long-term thinking	3.06
Ethical	3.87	Integrity/honest	3.06
Strategic	3.66	Humble	3.06
Collaborative	3.61	Good listener	3.06
High-performing/high-achieving	3.61	Collaborative	3.06

People often consider something a personality trait when it really isn't. For example, decision-making and communication (three identified in our list above from our studies) are not personality traits. These are learned behaviors and skills. Understanding the difference between core personality traits vs. behaviors that are malleable is critical. The further we are to the left or right on the continuum, the more difficult it becomes to modify behaviors. We either "go there" unconsciously and quickly, or it doesn't occur to us to behave in certain ways. These are typically major blind spots for us and are extremely difficult to change. This is where we need to be informed, educated, diligent, and honest in our assessment of folks.

and fired for lack of EQ, or emotional quotient, which is often used interchangeably with emotional intelligence. From a purist standpoint, emotional intelligence consists of four components: emotional regulation, self-awareness, trust, and empathy.

The results of our studies heavily emphasized the importance of EI. EI was very clearly identified as an essential component when considering personality in the global quantitative study. Still, even though it was not explicitly named in the criteria listings, it was named in many other ways by the CEOs in our study. In fact, EI was the biggest topic raised by CEOs during the interviews. Emotional intelligence (EI/EQ) was explicitly mentioned by 18 CEOs. In addressing EQ, people mentioned having intuition, tied IQ and EQ together, emphasized self-awareness, related it to humor, noted it as important for the ability to compromise, emphasized it was about finding ways to work together, and spoke of how this has become more important, and they have become more aware of its value over time. For many CEOs, the level of EQ was the most important indicator of potential.

To further this point, study participants spoke about emotional intelligence even when they did not know they were doing so. For example, an additional eleven leaders spoke of empathy...one of the four major components of EI. These eleven bring the total number of CEOs focusing on emotional intelligence to 29.

Additional comments included:

- "I'm always looking for people with strong empathetic skills." – Bill Winters, CEO, Standard Charter Bank
- "Empathy is more important than I mentioned so far." – Carel Nolte, CEO, CN&CO
- "I think that people that are genuine, people that have empathy, people that are real and not giving you a script all the time is critical. All those softer qualities to me are what I put more emphasis on, as opposed to 'can you tell me the revenue of every customer in this particular region?'" – John Holmes, CEO, AAR
- "Empathy is a critical component for success at any level. If you cannot relate to, understand, simply empathize with those around you—be it team members or customers, you are at a severe disadvantage." – Julia Stewart, CEO, Alurx
- "I'm asking, are these people not only listening to what's happening around them in the world but are they listening with a

level of empathy that suggests they know how to account for that. Not everybody knows how to do that." – Tim Kilpin, CEO, PlayMonster

- "Empathy. They have to be able to relate to the teams they are leading." – Bill Hewitt, CEO, Aternity
- "They need to have a strong degree of EI, including self-awareness." – Alison Croke, CEO, Wood River Health Services
- "I think you have to be humble and empathetic. Particularly over the last year, if you were an empathetic leader, it was probably a lot better for you and everyone who works for you." – Clayton Adams, CEO, Mascoma Savings Bank
- "I would say a key is emotional intelligence and ability to be able to ignite passion in people for them to follow you to achieve their own ultimate goals and the organizational goals. It's the ability within the person to be able to bring out the best in other people. That to me is leadership potential, that you've got the emotional intelligence, the ability to lead others and to bring the best out of others." – Kevin Chaplin, CEO, SA Ubuntu Foundation & Amy Foundation

The lack of emotional intelligence is apparent everywhere in the workplace. Here are five examples we have personally witnessed:

- A head of HR was neurotic and lacked all components of EI – no self-control, self-awareness, nor empathy. Consequently, no one trusted her. Her staff hated her, and many on her team or other areas in the company left the organization. Her lack of EI derailed the people's agenda within the organization.
- A brilliant industry expert was extremely cautious and risk averse. He lacked the ability to see himself as others did and failed spectacularly at his C-suite job.
- A senior-level executive convinced himself that the current issues were not him (lack of self-awareness) even though he had become quite volatile in his reactions many times (lack of self-control).
- A CEO lost the trust of his team due to a true lack of awareness of how his behaviors have created major trust issues and is about to lose half his team if things don't change.
- A well-known athletic trainer and his incredibly narcissistic wife lacked empathy for anything other than making money which created discord with clients such that clients came and left shortly afterwards for years.

Michael Levy, CEO, Crow Holdings, shared a personal example of the evolution of his emotional intelligence:

> I think there's a notion around compassion that is important. When I was going up through my career, I became the CEO of a public company when I was in my early 30s, and I have already had the benefit of Stephen Covey's work. I was doing my best to improve my craft. But I don't think I had enough sensitivity at the time. I ended up having more emphasis around the individual values of individual people. So, because I worked my ass off, I valued those who worked their ass off, which wasn't necessarily fair.

Related to the EI conversation is the concept of humility. Some CEOs, whom we admire and deem extremely successful, emphasized humility. A few examples included:

- "I would say to really junior people if you can demonstrate that you can do a job a level above you and do that with humility, and when you show you have questions and are paying attention, people will notice you." – Mary Dillon, CEO, Ulta Beauty. Mary further emphasized: "Ambition is important in leadership, but humility is also important for leadership. To me, the best leaders are ones that have a balance of both, and it can be hard to find, but it is super important."
- "If I had to choose a single attribute that straddles across all of these and is a predictor of future potential more than anything else, it is humility. Humility is a level of self-awareness and not taking yourself too seriously. Because if you're humble, you listen, and you're curious. If you're humble, you're congruent. If you're humble, you're always respectful, and so on. Humility is probably one of the most important values I look for." – Niren Chaudhary, CEO, Panera Bread.

In the previous chapter, you may recall that the idea of too much intelligence was raised as a concern by several CEOs when discussing intelligence as a criterion. What is interesting here is that the issue is not too much intelligence. The issue is actually a lack of emotional intelligence. People deemed "too intelligent" often demonstrate a significant lack of awareness in how they are showing up to others. They often struggle to empathize with others and find it difficult to control or regulate themselves, such as quickly getting deeply involved in a topic. All these elements can negatively impact on building a trusting relationship.

As practitioners, we see this a great deal. People misdiagnose what they see, such as in this case, but recognize it as an issue. The problem with that is, without clarity around what you are seeing, it is difficult to assess whether it is a dynamic that can be changed or not.

The good news about emotional intelligence is that it can be developed. Developing EI would require grinding to be able to develop competence in that area. It takes hard work to become more self-aware, it takes hard work to maintain self-control (especially for us redheads). To immerse yourself in someone else's experience is hard work, and to have a consistent set of behaviors that create a trusting relationship is not a walk in the park. However, if these are indeed deficiencies, they can be so significant that they can implode people's career aspirations.

Related to the discussion of emotional intelligence is chemistry because of the association with the idea of connecting with folks. Thirteen CEOs specifically identified chemistry as a critical factor when discussing personality. Chemistry is about personality and whether the combinations of personalities will work well together. CEOs talked about fit, collegial behavior, being able to connect and work together, being respectful, culture fit, needing to mesh, attitude, how well they work together, having shared/aligned values, and wanting someone that the team will like and trust.

Some illustrative comments included:

- "I've never hired anybody I don't like." – John Holmes, CEO, AAR
- "There is not a personality type I'm looking for. There's a type of chemistry I'm looking for. I don't care if somebody is introverted or extroverted or what their interests are in life. I care that they can collaborate with us, respect other people's opinions, and have the emotional intelligence to know how to work with their peers to get a better solution. To me, that sort of personality type, I guess, or an aspect of personality that I look at." – Mary Dillon, CEO, Ulta Beauty
- "I like to share a meal with a candidate to see how they treat other people in the normal course of their lives." – Bill Hewitt, CEO, Aternity
- For one CEO, chemistry trumps technical requirements, and they use psychometric testing to assist in determining a chemistry match. "Someone can be the most technical person but if they do not fit well with the team dynamic...they will not be a strong asset to this

specific part of the team." – David Hurwitz, CEO, Transaction Capital

- "What I'm looking for in personality is someone that's going to get along with the rest of our team and make a positive impact." – unnamed CEO, biotechnology firm
- "People who other people want to follow; you can see it. It's not just likeability. Although important, people want to follow someone because of who they are and how they engage. That can come across one of a thousand ways. They can be incredibly cerebral and really bright or really funny, but that element of people who want to follow someone and want to be in their company is essential." – Michael Levy, CEO, Crow Holdings
- "I operate really on a basis of trust. I really look for people from the first instance, or anything, but I feel like I can trust them and that we have shared values. It's very important to me." – Christelle Colman, CEO, Elite Risk Acceptances

Matt Barrie, Chief Executive of Freelancer.com, offered the following example of this concept.

> If you think about a two-by-two matrix, where on one axis you have performance or talent and the other axis you have cultural fit, you're always trying to hire the candidate with high talent and great cultural fit – and you'd never hire a candidate with low talent and poor attitude. Those that have a great attitude and low performance – well you invest in these people to bring their skills up. The tricky candidate is the one who is incredibly talented that is a really bad cultural fit. It's very difficult, but you need to fire these people immediately. I've got a classic example of this – there was a guy who joined us, and he was a university medalist in computer science, PhD. He did great work, and was always getting his work done on time, every time, but he would get it done so quickly that, you know, Monday morning 11 o'clock, he would sit there in the middle of the office playing a ukulele and watching cat videos on Reddit and be incredibly disruptive to everyone that was sitting around him. Next thing you know you'd have half a dozen lower-performance people crowding around the cat videos auditioning for his band. His team lead struggled to manage him because he was highly talented and always had the excuse that he had done all that was expected of him. His behavior eventually dragged a lot of people around him down and eventually turned them toxic. As hard as it may be, you always need to cut the high performers with bad attitudes.

Diversity. Diversity was a major topic for many CEOs and, based on our chapter on bias, is a bit related to chemistry and fit. Thirteen CEOs emphasized that many personality types will work for leaders and work well to promote diversity.

- "It is okay, even preferable, to have different personality types in an organization and direct report structure. Real leadership includes mastering the ability to bring the best out of a variety of people and bring different people together with common goals. To do this effectively, it us helpful to identify an inspiring shared vision while recognizing when you may need to morph your own personality to drive, coach, or meet the developmental needs of the people who report to you." – Sharon Price John, CEO, Build-A-Bear Workshop, Inc.
- "The more different, the better." – John Miller, CEO, Denny's
- "I've always tried in the management team that I've pulled together to have an extremely diverse range of personalities, and it makes it harder to manage." – Bill Winters, CEO, Standard Charter Bank
- "Earlier in my career as Sr. VP at Taco Bell, I was tasked with developing an entire training program that focused on identifying, interviewing, and hiring people from diverse backgrounds. What we found was an enormous tendency for those hiring to select candidates similar to themselves. This 'likeness hiring' can be a true barrier to achieving real diversity." – Julia Stewart, CEO, Alurx
- "Need someone who is able to handle diversity – comfortable with and see it as a strength to work with people of difference." – Carel Nolte, CEO CN&CO

Niël Pretorius, CEO of DRDGold Limited, offered an honest view about the ongoing challenges of actively sourcing and engaging people who are different from you.

> We don't intuitively look for leaders outside of our circle of comfort. We preach diversity, but we find it hard to practice it because I don't think we fully understand it and what it involves. It's not in the sense that we are politically incorrect, or being intentionally offensive, but I still think it is hard for a white male to interview a very young black female. We don't have a shared background, so there is a risk that, best intentions notwithstanding, you may come across as derogatory or racist or patronizing because of the language used. There is the potentiality for being insensitive and not even being aware of it, and it can be challenging to find ways to move forward.

Other leaders spoke of the culture being a mirror impacted by the personalities of the most senior leaders. David Hurwitz, CEO, Transaction Capital, illustrates this idea with the following comment:

> Our diversity comes to some extent, from a historic position where people were disadvantaged, to remain in the country, and the government is trying to put that back together. It's not like in the rest of the world where people are saying, 'we need gender diversity and race diversity over here.' We're saying there's a historical wrong that needs to be corrected. That is something that I've found quite difficult in South Africa.

Derailers: A Critical Focus for the Personality Conversation

Derailers – what to look for. Ten CEOs spoke about the concern of derailing attributes. Derailers are unacceptable elements including personality traits such as condescending, obnoxious, rude, negative, blaming others, ineffective communicators, entirely socially awkward, extroverts who are "all over the place," people who cannot focus, or those who are narcissistic.

Here is a critical point. Our biggest concern or interest relating to personality is in the area of derailers.

Too many times, people are mistakenly hired or promoted because managers did one of three things.

1. They missed the behaviors.
2. They didn't recognize the impact of the behaviors; or
3. They thought they could either manage or change the behaviors.

To be fair, this is a tricky space. Because most people are not behaviorists and do not have the training or psychological insight to understand what they are witnessing.

Additionally, many dark side traits – as referred to by Hogan and Hogan – are attributes that often catch people's attention and get them promoted! Narcissists are much more likely to be employed as managers, particularly since they have a strong interest early in their careers to be leaders (Nuzulia & Why, 2020). There are three dark personality genres – narcissism, Machiavellianism, and psychopathy. Many narcissists, for example, are very charismatic, and many psychopathic tendencies are associated with being charming and entertaining. Focusing on less extreme examples of dark side behaviors, examples of personality traits that were of concern were ones that fell into all the dimensions of the Hogan derailer scale, the dark side of personality. Those were reserved, prudent, imaginative, bold, colorful, skeptical, diligent, excitable, cautious, mischievous, and leisurely. These characteristics often demonstrate a lack of concern or regard for others, and it is the mistrust they generate that creates issues in organizations. Hostility in these types often creates a significant negative impact on the organization, not only for the ones directly involved but for everyone watching, which often leads to high employee turnover, low engagement, lack of decision-making, etc.

Let's look at how our CEOs spoke of certain concerning behaviors that fell into these categories.

Reserved

- "If you have a personality type that is not effective at communicating, then that would be a problem." – Austin Allison, CEO, Pacaso
- "Introverted people are fine; they do not make leaders in the sense that we talk about leadership potential – with the ability to lead people to bring out the best." – Kevin Chaplin, CEO, SA Ubuntu Foundation & Amy Foundation. Also, from Kevin on this topic, "Extrovert who is all over the place, isn't good with focus and detail doesn't make a good leader."
- "If you can't communicate to people and get them to understand what that vision is and get them to want to march to the same drum, they become a difficult leader." – Tom O'Mara, CEO, Eligius Advisory, LLC
- "Someone not completely socially awkward." – Alison Croke. CEO, Wood River Health Services

Imaginative

- One brilliant CEO is known to pile on with new ideas in every conversation every day such that the team cannot keep up and have become resentful.

- Another CEO engages in what the team calls "magical thinking" when it comes to the realities of executing something, often "defying the laws of logic, time, space and whatever suits his needs at the time."

Skeptical

- "I really don't respect people I perceive to look for external factors for why something is the way it is, as opposed to internal factors." – Coco Brown, CEO, The Athena Alliance
- "If they're a very negative person, consistently view things through a negative lens, or put people down then this will eventually be apparent in their conversations. These are the kind of red flags I'll look for when someone's talking. It's often independent of the subject matter." – Samir Patel, CEO, Moonlight Therapeutics, Inc.
- "A personality that is negative would be a challenge for me." – Carel Nolte, CEO CN&CO

Bold

- "You hope not to bring someone on that has a narcissistic bent to them." – Alison Croke, CEO Wood River Health Services
- A leader who becomes bored with the content easily often doesn't let presenters get past the first page or two before taking over the meeting.

Colorful

- "I definitely don't want to see someone who thinks everything is perfect because rarely is that the case." – Samir Patel, CEO, Moonlight Therapeutics, Inc.
- An executive laughs loudly and excessively long at almost every joke.
- One executive is known for constantly having side-bar conversations in meetings and that is after coming in late and stopping to say hello to everyone on her way to her seat, including getting a snack and drink.

Excitable

- "The things that alarm me are certain behaviors – rude, obnoxious, duplicity, self-serving." – Jyoti Gupta, CEO, Volk Optical
- One leader is simply known for yelling when he is frustrated regardless of who is in the room.
- Another leader falls in love with every idea and, in his enthusiasm for these ideas, attempts to pull the organization off track to garner support. He averaged 10 new ideas that he distracts the organization with, much to their distress.

The Hogan framework is very useful in showing how some of these are more detrimental or toxic than others. Hogan's premise is certain behaviors often surface in times of stress, such as deadlines, extreme fatigue, hunger, etc., causing further issues. They consider these strong characteristics ones that should be "watch-outs."

We, the authors, see a whole suite of behaviors in people during interviews or throughout the workplace that are red flags for putting them in any type of management or leadership role. Examples of potential derailing behaviors:

- Arrogance, lacking humility
- Hostility – this one is clear and shows up subtly and directly both verbally and in behaviors
- Extreme introversion or low sociability, lacking the ability to connect well with people
- Extreme self-focus, lacking any sense of community
- Extreme independence, lacking a team orientation
- Extremely negative, discerning, or skeptical
- Extreme detail and process orientation resulting in tremendous difficulty navigating change or adapting to changing circumstances
- Extreme conservativism or low risk-taking which limits the ability to advance or grow
- Poor communication skills – talks too much, talks without awareness of audience, incoherence resulting in lack of ability to create engagement
- Too abstract or high level resulting in limited ability to translate ideas into action

- Polarizing or selfish behaviors resulting in lack of ability to create followership
- Dishonest or lacking the ability to create trust
- Significant lack of confidence or lacking the ability to get results or buy-in
- Lack of curiosity resulting in being surface level in the conceptualization of ideas
- Lack of emotional intelligence

The derailer idea is the most critical element of the personality discussion.

How to Assess It?

We probed the CEOs to further understand how they assess for it, and a sampling of comments are below:

- "Even with the assessment and understanding more about personality, it's really still important to understanding where their strengths are and where can we recognize that there's going to be some uncomfortable areas where we just have to make sure we're investing in their training, their development. And getting them more comfortable in those uncomfortable positions." – Brian Cornell, CEO, Target
- "I do look at people's social media, how they're engaged with the world using social media." – Carel Nolte, CEO, CN&CO
- "I assess by spending time with them." – Coco Brown, CEO, The Athena Alliance
- "We have an internal coach for the executives. We also use external coaches in certain instances." – David Hurwitz, CEO, Transaction Capital
- "I give them scenarios and see how they react, typically as an interview question just to assess personality." – Sharad Joshi, CEO, Satio, Inc.
- "Myers–Briggs Assessment is a common tool which I have used at the executive level at numerous companies. It helps paint a more complete picture of the individual and how they will fit within the team and the overall organization." – Julia Stewart, CEO, Alurx

- "I tend to ask a lot of questions about things which are not related to work, like what do you do in your free time, achievements, aspirations, hobbies, interests? This helps me understand the personality better than business achievements." – Alessandro Felici, CEO, Evlonet
- "It's really important that, whether I'm in the boardroom or on the barstool next to somebody, I want to be able to interact with them. I want them to be exactly who they are, their authentic selves, and I want to enjoy that individual as much as possible." – Trey Sutten, CEO, Cardinal Innovations Healthcare
- First of all, I ask them to write me a cover letter, and you can see in the words that they use typically who they are. So that's number one. Then...I ask questions that will try to smoke out the BS answers." – Patrick McMullan, CEO, Three Square Market
- One CEO asks questions about things nothing to do with work, such as hobbies, achievements, interests, etc. The intent was to hear how they talked about such things and to assess whether there was an element of negativity. "It's not necessarily about the content of the subject and their thought process. This is what gives me some insight into a person's personality." – Samir Patel, CEO, Moonlight Therapeutics, Inc.

The second most popular method for assessing personality was through the use of assessment tools. In the global study, 40% of participants identified assessments as their preferred method. The Hogan Executive Assessments were referenced several times, even with Brian Cornell, the CEO of Target, mentioning at the start of our interview, "Just now before our interview, I was just actually grabbing a file with some Hogan assessments." Others mentioned Myers–Briggs, the PAPI, the Predictive Index (PI) either as an indicator of potential, an indicator to question and learn more about someone based on an extreme tendency, or to assist in engaging with leaders.

Other methods referenced were word of mouth from others or references, having conversations with stakeholders, and feedback from others.

Summary and Recommended Path Forward

In our practical and research-based opinion, personality is the trickiest criterion for people to properly assess. They are less likely to say personality is important and are more inclined to talk about chemistry, emotional intelligence, and specific personality attributes. We need to break the barrier on the taboo in talking about personality because, in our experience, it is the biggest derailer of leadership success. You hear it in the top reasons why people leave organizations – the relationship with their manager. It's just far too common to be a coincidence, and the research points to personality.

The big idea regarding personality is to be honest and *really* watch out for derailing personality traits. Some are clear and overt. However, many are insidious but not less significant in how people operate. The other *big* idea related to personality is emotional intelligence. Become an EQ Czar on the topic. People are being hired for IQ and fired for EQ all over the place...for good reason. This can be a tremendous source of improvement in picking the right leaders from the start.

If you are truly serious, start with these steps:

1. Don't hire someone you think you are going to "fix" or "develop" when they come on board because you have observed some concerning elements on how they operate.
2. Become a Jedi interviewer. Ask a ton of questions to get to the understory. People reveal themselves in spite of their attempts to conceal components of their true selves.
3. Use personality assessments to determine how strong preferences are...both in terms of people leaning towards something or far away from something. These instruments can give you great insights on where to probe further. Behavior trumps assessments, but largely the assessments can tell you how strong the gravitational pull is for someone one way or the other.
4. Learn to meet people where they are and cherish the diversity of your team. A diverse team takes more work and more time to get to results, in most instances. The returns are worth it. However, don't mistake bad behavior or derailing personality traits as "different styles." We don't need to tolerate elements that erode a team's success in the spirit of diversity.
5. Become a brilliant detective of derailing personality traits. For example, someone who is detail oriented and wants to do good work is a real asset. Someone who is so stuck in the detail and a perfectionist is taking those strengths too far and they become impediments. Such persons would not make good leaders. Become skilled

at deciphering what is a behavior that can be slightly modified and what is hard-wiring that an act of God would be required for it to change.

6. Explore personality assessments and find a favorite. Ours is the Hogan and the DiSC.

7. Bring this into what you talk about with your team. Focus on behaviors, but when a strong pattern of negative or limiting behaviors does not change, you need to make a change and certainly don't promote them.

8. Check out our website for good interview questions, including ones on emotional intelligence.

Visit **determiningleadershippotential.com** for case studies and additional resources.

Reference List

Church, A., & Ezama, S. (2020, April 1). PepsiCo's formula for leadership potential. Association for Talent Development. www.td.org/magazines/td -magazine/pepsicos-formula-for-leadership-potential

De Bruin, V. (2012). The relationship between mixed model emotional intelligence and personality. *South African Journal of Psychology, 42*(4), 532–542.

Le Sante, D. R., Eaton, A. A., & Viswesvaran, C. (2021). How contextual performance influences perceptions of personality and leadership potential. *Journal of Work and Organizational Psychology, 37*(2), 93–106.

Nuzulia, S., & Why, F. Y. P. (2020). When the dark shines: The role of dark personality traits in leadership role occupancy and hiring decisions in a collectivistic culture. *Social Psychological and Personality Science, 11*(8), 1089–1100.

8
What do We Mean by Motivation?

Kimberly Janson and Melody Rawlings

As we know by now, personality and intelligence are largely fixed. The two other components of the Leadership Blueprint, learning agility and motivation, both located in the Growth Dimension in the framework, require people to supply these qualities themselves. We don't control other people's level of motivation; they do. This chapter covers what it means to be motivated, why it's important, and what to look for in assessing motivation in others. It includes an overview of intrinsic and extrinsic motivation and a discussion of whose job it isn't to motivate employees. The punchline of this chapter is there is great power and tremendous return when you hire people who bring their own engines that propel them.

Motivation is the will and drive "to move" ourselves for our own reasons with great energy and passion. We do that when we want something which causes us to act. In short, motivation is a psychological process relating to the drive to achieve based on internal or external forces (Paais & Pattiruhu, 2020).

When people are motivated, they fully commit to being their best selves, and that presents in many ways. Brian Cornell, CEO, Target, shares that perspective with this comment,

> Going back to my time at PepsiCo, and really going back to the late 90s, I was introduced to the corporate athlete program. It had a profound impact on me. I started to really embrace the program and understand how important things like rest, nutrition, and exercise were for being a high-performing executive. If you're in an executive position, having high learning agility, you must train like professional athletes. We need to invest in our health, wellness and especially invest in our energy, so that when we need to be at our best, we can be, and that's a byproduct.

DOI: 10.4324/9781003272212-8

Brian's comments are a terrific example of the power of someone who is highly motivated.

What does it look like? Our CEOs described motivation in a variety of ways that included:

- Initiative, energy level – "It's what leadership is about quite honestly. I think to be a great leader, you've got to bring your own engine." – Dick Johnson, CEO, Foot Locker
- Intentionality, the ability to create followership, such as this quote by Austin Allison, CEO, Pacaso, "It's hard to want to follow somebody that's not motivated."
- For some, it is a combination of things as mentioned by John Lawlor, CEO, Maugel Architects, with this quote, "We prescribe the Jim Collins Good to Great framework – disciplined people, disciplined thought, disciplined action, and they're self-motivated."
- "Another example is someone saying, 'I can do more...give me a chance.' Inherently, I expect a high drive, high ambition, and high work ethic. I think those are sort of aspects of motivation, and I say that's a given." – Mary Dillon, CEO, Ulta Beauty
- "I look for people that have a real fire in their belly." – unnamed CEO, biotechnology firm
- "It's someone who wants to move forward. Some people want to move forward as part of a team, other people want to move a team forward. Both are great attributes that can move a company forward!" – Larry Schreiber, CEO, SanteFe Health Care, Inc.

Other descriptors CEOs used were based on motivation to do a good job such as: demonstrating entrepreneurial zeal, acting as the owner, coming up and wanting to "crush it," finding something to move the business ahead, follow-up, are self-starters, are purpose-driven, they value the work, they want to move forward, it shows how they work with others, shows in their pace, how they move, do they show up on time, do they go above and beyond, and are they prepared.

Wide Agreement on Its Importance

Self-motivated individuals are likely to be top performers:

- The self-motivated have a high return on investments made into them.

- They are self-motivated to succeed.
- Others may copy them.
- You can teach skills, but you can't teach self-motivation.
- You won't have to worry about employee engagement.

Importantly, for our purposes, highly motivated people are a clear indication of leadership potential. In fact, some early work ahead of the creation of the Leadership Blueprint found through surveying many companies that most leaders consider people who are very interested and motivated to advance their career exhibit a clear indicator of high potential. Additionally, highly motivated folks are more inclined to engage in developmental activities to make themselves better (Paais & Pattiruhu, 2020). Taking this concept to overall team performance, research has shown that when a team has people who are highly willing to engage in the job and invest to be successful…those folks account for approximately 40% of the team's success – just by themselves (Clark & Saxberg, 2019)!

In our own research studies, a few interesting trends emerged. In the global quantitative study, about 13% of participants identified motivation as a criterion when asked what criteria they use and were unprompted. When prompted and asked specifically as to whether they use motivation as a criterion, that number shot up to 86%. Compare that to the CEO study, where 52% of CEOs indicated they use motivation as a criterion, even when unprompted. But that number went to 100% when asked specifically if they use motivation! This information is represented in Figure 8.1. The first bar represents the number of times motivation was identified in the GDLP as a criterion to DLP when unprompted. The second bar indicates the percentage of participants in the GDLP who use personality as a criterion when prompted. The third and fourth bars reflect the same information for the CEO study.

When participants in the global quantitative study broke it down as to what they look for, participants in the global quantitative study identified the following in terms of what it looked like:

- Proactiveness (82%)
- Persistence (75%)
- Effort (70%)
- Focus (63%)
- Other (summary): commitment, resilience, drive.

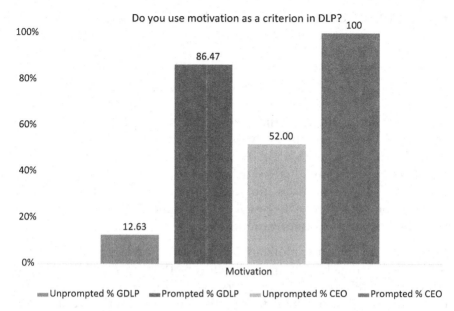

Figure 8.1 How CEOs use motivation as a DLP criterion. Figure created by authors.

Much of the discussion with the CEOs consisted of them reinforcing the notion that motivation was critical. Comments included sentiments such as:

- "Highly successful people motivate themselves and don't need me to do that. Winners motivate themselves." – Patrick McMullan, CEO, Three Square Market
- "It's going to be hard for someone to get ahead and excel in this organization if they do not demonstrate motivation and energy." – Clayton Adams, CEO, Mascoma Savings Bank
- "Individuals that have self-motivation and who are competitive are the ones that I've found to be the most successful leaders." – David Page, Chairman, The Swift Group
- "I think team members need an engine; they need motivation. That is not to be confused with capability. If I must choose between two candidates, one possesses a wealth of experience but little motivation and the other has a ton of motivation, but light on experience – I'll take the motivated person every time. Because at the end of the day, they have that tenacity, that grit, that desire that 'I'm going to go make it work.'" – Julia Stewart, CEO, Alurx

- "They have to be a self-starter. I'm lucky if I spend one hour a week one-on-one with my direct reports. They need to set their own agenda and determine how they should be spending their time. Must have personal ambition and drive. If not a self-starter, they will flame out pretty quickly." – Chip Bergh, CEO, Levi Strauss & Co

An important distinction...intrinsic or extrinsic motivation? You likely have heard the distinction between extrinsic and intrinsic motivation. According to Herzberg's 1959 Two-Factor Theory, two groups of factors determine an individual's satisfaction or dissatisfaction (Alshmemri et al., 2017). Extrinsic motivation comes from outside the person, resulting in some type of social reward or punishment, and is less likely to contribute toward real motivation.

People with the intrinsic motivations will work tirelessly to keep improving and achieving. They will give herculean effort...a great deal of extra effort, often referred to as discretionary effort, towards these desired outcomes. People working 9 am to 5 pm will give you the requirements of the job, but the folks who are then working 5 pm to 9 pm are giving you their discretionary effort and often their passion. Two studies of large banks in the USA found that those who are intrinsically motivated are better performers, have lower stress/anxiety/depression, feel greater satisfaction with work, and often enjoy better physical health (Adair, 2009).

When the work itself carries the value for you, such as achievement, recognition, variety, and creativity, that is intrinsic motivation. It centers on the activity or work being the reward. People intrinsically motivated are always challenging themselves. You recognize these people easily. When the work is a means to a result, and the result is what holds value, that is extrinsic motivation. It's externally directed and comes from some type of outside pressure such as a deadline, fear, performance reviews, etc.

All of this basically answers the question, "why do we do what we do?"

Many of our CEOs spoke about the importance of people being intrinsically motivated. One common reason provided was that external motivators will run their course. A sampling of their offerings on the subject are featured below:

- "Motivation is important, and it's important that you're internally motivated. When you're externally motivated, there comes a tipping point where you either have enough incentive to move on, or you say, 'you know what...there's just no incentive to continue,' but when you're internally motivated, it's as if there's nothing that will really stand in your way." – Keith Herman, CEO, IPA Equities

- In a similar way but emphasizing that it is best when there are a few motivators, Jandel T. Allen-Davis, CEO, Craig Hospital, said: "You got to be motivated by something, and hopefully you're motivated by the right things as a leader or just a person in an organization. I hope it's a mission and the work. It can't just be motivated by a paycheck and, frankly, can't just be motivated by the mission. It's the constellation of a bunch of different things."
- One CEO was explicit in the direct link of motivation to potential:, "If someone is not intrinsically motivated, I find it hard to see how they have potential. If you need to direct somebody to be motivated to do something, if the person is not a self-starter, then that's not good. If you're talking about if somebody can also be extremely motivated by money or if he gets the right amount of money, he's motivated, then that is not the right motivation. It only works so far. I'm hiring new people and they focus too much on the package, I get skeptical." – Robin van Rozen, CEO, Glen Dimplex Consumer Appliance

How to Assess It?

Motivation level was assessed in a variety of ways by CEOs (10), with observation being the top choice with these study participants.

- Keith Herman, CEO, IPA Equities, emphasized that "words are just words, and it's your actions that mean everything."
- Norman Soutar, CEO, William Jackson Food Group, indicated they measure it based on individuals' response and performance in not-so-fun placements or less than ideal situations and ultimately how committed they are.
- Sharad Joshi, CEO, Satio Inc., uses open-ended questions that often have nothing to do with work during the interview process to assess motivation.
- Siobhan Dullea, CEO, MassChallenge, said she recognizes it when people come with ideas and ask for more. She also offered that it looks like this, "Comes with ideas, not problems, and asking for more, whether it's more information, more context, or more

responsibility. Has the motivation to produce high-quality work and not producing work that is below the expected standards. Aims to produce something better than what people anticipate."

- Resiliency was also mentioned as a defining characteristic of motivation by Siobhan Dullea, CEO, MassChallenge.
- Victor Velazquez, Executive Director (CEO), Maryland State Bar Association, indicated they know it when they look at the background of candidates – did they solve big problems, demonstrate a big appetite, overcome some challenges, history, education, successes, etc.
- You can also detect the absence of motivation, as indicated by this comment by Mary Dillon, CEO, Ulta Beauty: "I might see in a very junior person a lot of potential, but they may be of the mindset, 'I don't want to work that hard all my life,' or 'I don't want to give that much of my life up.'"
- "Someone who really has the initiative and ambition to want to improve something on a continuous basis and the drive to want to continue to win. I've got some company values that I have created over time. One of them is Take Charge. One of them is What Can I Improve Today? Another one I've stolen from Reed Hastings from Netflix, which is We're Not a Happy Family, We're a Pro Sports Team. You want to have the best players on the bench at all times. It's really someone who has the go-get attitude that just wants to build a better world...I talk about building a better life. It's through process and services, we really do that with Freelancer. We look for someone who wants to actually change the world and change the future through helping entrepreneurs around the world create innovative products and services. This is what almost 60 million of our customers do on Freelancer. We look for people with ambition." – Matt Barrie, Chief Executive of Freelancer.com
- Trey Sutten, CEO, Cardinal Innovations Healthcare, referenced it this way: "The way that I experienced it is general urgency. When I think about motivation, I think about wanting to change the world positively. I only have so many years and so many days and hours to do that....Urgency is probably the first sign where I'll ask if something was done....The other way I see it is on the positive side is when people bring things to me: new pilots, new ideas, and new ways of doing business. That's kind of the positive experience that I have or the positive way I experienced motivation."

The concept of ambition was raised nine times by the CEOs in relation to motivation.

- A representative comment was offered by Coco Brown, CEO, The Athena Alliance: "I think a lot of leadership potential comes from internal ambition and a bit of a sense of gnosis (knowledge). You must both be compelled to do whatever it is you are setting out for and *know* (beyond believing) that you can achieve it. I think those two things are incredibly important." This was associated with the concept of being a self-starter and trial by fire.
- Mary Dillon, CEO, Ulta Beauty, expounded on the importance of motivation and how she saw it, especially as a woman. "I admire ambition. I'm an ambitious woman, and I hate when people use that word negatively, especially about women. Ambition is important in leadership, but humility is also important for leadership. To me, the best leaders are ones that have a balance of both."
- Matt Barrie, Chief Executive of Freelancer.com, said they "know ambition because it is in someone who wants to change the world."

Seven CEOs expressed that too much ambition and motivation is as troublesome as not enough.

- Joel Stevenson, CEO, Yesware, indicated that having "extreme motivation and has no work–life balance won't work as we tend to have a good balance here. Someone who is too much out of balance would be tough to handle."
- Nachi Junankar, CEO, Avrio AI, expressed concern about being too full of themselves when it relates to ambition and "filling a hole in themselves."
- Vineet Kumar, CEO, Intellyk Inc., spoke of the essential need that motivations were aligned with organizational need and cautioned about growing a culture that only focuses on and rewards people growing fast.

Leader's Role

One of the confusing elements about employee motivation is the volumes of literature relating to the manager being responsible for "motivating their employees." This concept is tremendously misunderstood and can be quite detrimental to an organization's success. Managers and leaders should not be responsible for motivating employees. Truly, they can't. That is a choice and a lifestyle that someone chooses for themselves. The countless times we have heard leaders say something to the effect, "He's really good in this area, but if I could just get him motivated to..." Stop right here – hard stop. You can't. So, stop trying.

Melody shares this powerful example of motivation. "At my former university, 'opportunities' were offered only to tenured faculty and not others. I was once in a faculty meeting and the department chair asked for a volunteer to lead a specific committee. I raised my hand and there was this awkward silence that felt like it went on for ever. She finally said, 'Well, thank you, but I would actually like someone who is on tenure-track to take that role.' Needless to say, I felt completely demotivated and never volunteered again. Because of what happened, coming to Northcentral University has been a breath of fresh air with amazing opportunities that would never have been available to me at the former. Because I was treated as fully capable and responsible, I have always felt very motivated at NCU."

A challenge is that most hiring managers, and HR recruiting managers, mistake enthusiasm for the role and the desire to be hired for motivation. Honestly assessing for motivation, which is at the core of strong potential, needs a concerted effort to achieve success.

Summary and Recommended Path Forward

This seems like an obvious selection criterion but look around the workplace. We have many people but, more importantly and concerningly, many managers who would not be described as high motivation. Why do we tolerate such things? Our working theory is we have relied on technical expertise and performance as our lens and are willing to settle. "Not everyone is looking to be the super star" is a variation of what is said when someone is lacking motivation. Our response...why not? If someone wants to be the fry cook for life..., wouldn't you want them to have great energy and drive, and commitment to be a great fry cook. Why wouldn't we demand that of our leaders?

The other curiosity is that conversation about the manager's role in motivating others. Let's be very clear again – it is not our job, nor can we be successful in motivating others. The number of articles available with a title similar to "Learn How to Motivate Your Employees" adds to the lack of clarity on this issue. Harvard published one to the tune of "How to Motivate Your Problem Employees." Sigh...just no. People must choose that for themselves. We, as leaders, should be clearing away the debris that is unnecessarily in the way so people can go faster with greater ease.

Let's take that further. You have two horsewomen, your authors. You simply cannot make a horse drink who doesn't want to do so. The closest is to get a turkey baster or tube and squeeze it down their throats. It's ugly, dramatic, lots comes back at you, and you get covered, and it's often ineffective. You can add electrolytes to their water buckets, so it tastes good and the water they use is processed more efficiently, but they still won't drink if they don't want to. Wouldn't it be easier if you had a horse that was a good drinker? Yes. The answer is yes. If this was a "thing," it would be on the list of things you assess when evaluating the show jumper you are thinking about buying...X-rays, scope, disposition, water-drinking ability...right? Seems clear with horses. It's as clear with people, we just haven't treated it the same.

If you are truly serious, start with these steps:

1. Learn to look for true motivation and not motivation just to get a job. Truly get to know people to understand them more fully.
2. People have preferences and are more inclined to move towards things that appeal to them. Become proficient in a tool like the DiSC to understand a person's preferences to help you distill what are communication disconnects versus true lack of motivation.
3. Calculate the return you get from employees who are giving you their discretionary efforts...you know...5 pm to 9 pm and weekends. It is usually a pretty significant ROI.
4. Be courageous and do the right thing for your team by eliminating low or average performers, especially those who are low in motivation.
5. Be clear on the metrics by which we evaluate motivation. Ones that emerged in the studies were proactiveness, persistence, effort, focus, resilience, commitment, and others. What are the four or five factors you will use on your scorecard for this?
6. Elements often surrounding highly motivated people are energy, optimism, and confidence. Look for these as indirect indicators of motivation.

7. It is hard to assess in interviews, so to do this to the best degree, hone your questioning. Here are sample questions that can surface clues to one's motivational levels:
   - Describe a time when you recognized you weren't going to be able to meet multiple deadlines. What did you do about it? What was the outcome?
   - Tell me about a time when you had an idea that was great for your own work, your team, or your company. How did you get your management/peers excited about it? How did you follow through to ensure your idea came to life?
   - When you're able to take extra time in your role, do you ever do anything to make your job easier or more efficient?
   - What techniques have you learned or discovered that make your job easier or make you more productive?
   - What motivates you to go to work every day?
   - Tell me about a time where you went above and beyond your role and expectations. Why did you do this? What exactly did you do?
   - If you find yourself stuck doing repetitive work, how do you motivate yourself to continue and complete it?
   - Have you ever been a part of an unmotivated team? What did you do to stay motivated and make work interesting?
   - What is your biggest dream in life?
   - What goals, including career goals, have you set for the next five years? How about for your whole life?
   - How would you define success in your career?
   - What roles do your manager and team play in your motivation at work?
   - In your experience, what motivates your best on-the-job performance?
   - Have you ever had a manager/peer who created a toxic workplace? What actions did you take to motivate yourself and others, despite the toxicity?
   - Describe the work environment that makes you most productive and/or happy.
   - What's one idea you think we could implement today that would make employees more excited to come to work tomorrow?
   - Think back to the worst work environment you've been a part of. What about it made it a terrible place to work? How would you make it a better place to work?
   - What makes you want to leave your current role?

- What could your current company change about your job, your team, or their culture to keep you on their team?
- How would you define a healthy balanced life? At what point do you think it's necessary to blur the lines?
- Describe how a previous manager motivated you to perform at the highest level.
- What were the specific actions your manager took to motivate you?
- How would you motivate those who report to you?
- Evaluate what makes you feel that you've had a successful week at work?
- How do you respond when things are not going well at work?

Visit **determiningleadershippotential.com** for case studies and additional resources.

Reference List

Adair, J. E. (2009). *Leadership and motivation: The fifty–fifty rule and the eight key principles of motivating others.* Kogan Page, Philadelphia, PA.

Alshmemri, M., Shahwan-Akl, L., & Maude, P. (2017). Herzberg's two-factor theory. *Life Science Journal, 14*(5), 12–16.

Clark, R. E., & Saxberg, B. (2019, March 13). 4 reasons good employees lose their motivation. *Harvard Business Review.* https://hbr.org/2019/03/4-reasons-good-employees-lose-their-motivation

Paais, M., & Pattiruhu, J. R. (2020). Effect of motivation, leadership, and organizational culture on satisfaction and employee performance. *The Journal of Asian Finance, Economics, and Business, 7*(8), 577–588.

9
What do We Mean by Learning Agility?

Kimberly Janson and Melody Rawlings

The more and varied experiences people have and the more knowledge someone must pull from and apply to situations and problems, the more effective they are. All this experience gathering is fueled by learning agility. If one does not have a high learning agility, the rest doesn't matter. This chapter provides a deep dive into the meaning of learning agility, why it is important in determining leadership potential, and how to assess it. The chapter provides insight directly from the CEOs and the methods they use to identify learning agility in others, such as curiosity, adaptability, and desire to learn.

Learning agility is a visceral commitment to the ongoing acquisition of new knowledge and skills. People who have high learning agility:

- gravitate to new challenges, not only embrace but seek change
- are curious
- constantly challenge the status quo
- are goal- and achievement-oriented?
- apply critical thinking
- enjoy solving complex problems
- are problem-solvers but problem-finders that then allow them to solve those problems.

Their desire is insatiable, which is useful for their success because learning from experiences accelerates their effectiveness. Learning agility is about mindset. Someone's learning agility is identifiable by the demonstration of speed of assimilation and adaptability. Unlearning is an important but critical hallmark of those who are learning agile as well (Lasse, 2020).

DOI: 10.4324/9781003272212-9

Wide Agreement on Its Importance

It's simply a different world of work than what we knew even 10 years ago. Indeed, those who learn quickly stand a better chance of success. If that was not compelling enough, Korn Ferry's research (Knight & Wong, 2020) indicates:

- Companies who have executives with high learning agility have 25% higher profit margins than their peers!
- The research also indicated that learning agile leaders were five times more likely to be considered highly engaged leaders
- High learning agility leaders are promoted at twice the pace as those with a lower learning agility.
- A meta-analysis of twenty other studies that included 5,000 employees showed that learning agility was viewed as more important than resilience, executive presence, or cognitive skills.
- Another study reported 62% of respondents identified learning agility as the most important criterion (Harvey & De Meuse, 2021).
- Learning agility is so critical, it has been described as the difference between just surviving and thriving (Ellis, 2021) in the world of work.

The extensive research conducted that resulted in the Leadership Blueprint proved the dependability of learning agility in predicting leadership potential. In that study, more than half of the organizations known for being top companies for leadership development use a learning agility assessment to determine leadership potential (Harvey & De Meuse, 2021). Companies such as PepsiCo, Novartis, Mars, GE, and Mondelez have used learning agility for years (De Meuse, 2019). Through this work and other studies, it has been determined that relying on learning agility is more reliable than relying on performance.

Consider this – the findings of two studies showed that 71% of high performers are not high potentials! This is a big idea and a concerning one because it is often high performance that catches the eye of senior leaders, which leads to promotions...and significantly contributes to the issue of selecting the wrong person for leadership roles. Conversely, 93% of high potentials are high performers!

People with higher learning agility are 18 times more likely to be identified as having high potential (Ellis, 2021) than those with lower scores.

These same people typically outperform peers, learn new information quickly, learn how to interact quickly, get promoted more quickly, are provided the most sought-after opportunities for development, and derail less often (Hallenbeck, 2016). Not only are high potential leaders strong contributors, but they also create a positive impact on the organization through their ongoing commitment to excellence, then subsequently role model positive behaviors.

Syd Finkelstein is a dear colleague and an expert in the field. Kim met Syd when she created the Leadership Development program at Hasbro (referenced by CEO Sharon Price John in Chapter 5) in partnership with Tuck Business School and further partnered with Syd at Hasbro and with other clients. His hallmark work of *Why Smart Executives Fail* showed many attributes of executives who had exhibited habits that were far from having strong learning agility, starting with resistance to innovation and change and clinging to an inadequate view of reality. Kim also had the occasion to work extensively with Marshall Goldsmith both in that same Hasbro program she built with Tuck and in several capacities since as well. Marshall's iconic book, *What Got You Here Won't Get You There,* is the poster child for the need for learning agility. The signs of the power of learning agility are ubiquitous.

Our research supports the data confirming that it is a critical component of determining leadership potential. As indicated in Figure 9.1, when asked in the global quantitative study what criteria are used, only 11% of participants identified learning agility but when asked directly whether they use learning agility, that increased by 75 percentage points! In the CEO study, 38% of participants identified the criteria being used in the open question but that increased by 60 percentage points. In totality, 98% of CEOs indicated that learning agility was critical in determining leadership potential. The first bar represents the number of times learning agility was identified in the GDLP as a criterion to DLP when unprompted. The second bar indicates the percentage of participants in the GDLP who use personality as a criterion when prompted. The third and fourth bars reflect the same information for the CEO study.

What does It Look Like?

With the launch of learning agility through Lombardo and Eichinger's work (Harvey & De Meuse, 2021) learning agility has long been described as having initially four components: mental agility, people agility, change agility, and results agility.

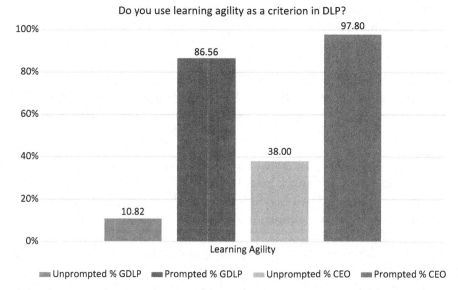

Figure 9.1 How CEOs use learning agility as a DLP criterion. Figure created by authors.

1. *Mental agility* – the ability to think critically about complex problems
2. *People agility* – understanding people and the ability to work effectively with people
3. *Change agility* – insatiable appetite for change
4. *Results agility* – ability to deliver results the first time, especially in critical situations.

Importantly – later research added *self-awareness* as a fifth dimension to the definition of learning agility.

5. *Self-awareness* – understanding of our own strengths and weaknesses and the ongoing solicitation of feedback to enable the quest to always be better (Buckner & Marberry, 2018; Ellis, 2021; Finkelstein et al., 2018; Knight & Wong, 2020).

In the global study, we asked participants to identify what they looked for in terms of learning agility using the traditional five components. The results are as follows:

- Change agility 77%
- Self-awareness 74%

- People agility 70%
- Mental agility 57%
- Results agility 53%

Curiosity (similar to mental agility). The most common association of learning agility, detected through the comments of ten CEOs, was to link learning agility to curiosity. Some describe it as a cycle of curiosity, and others expressed appreciation for it, such as,

- "I do like people that are curious. I think a measure of that is outside interest. I think people who collect things, have a hobby, sports, or have some outside interest to show it's not all about work and kids. I like the unique qualities about people." – John Holmes, CEO, AAR
- Several described the curiosity component simply as the inclination to explore new ideas and challenge oneself.
    - "I think it's exploring new ideas. Part of being a leader is having the confidence and curiosity to, what we've coined as, place bets. In other words, don't always do the status quo and challenge yourself and your teams to think differently. Put some proposals on the table for how we could do things differently, and not fearing failure, in fact, learning from it." – Frank Roe, CEO, SmartBear Software
- Another CEO spoke about curiosity everywhere – manufacturing facility/boardroom/military, etc.
    - "I think you have to because the world – whether you are talking about leadership in the military, leadership in a manufacturing facility, leadership in a boardroom, you have to have that learning agility because it's the only way that you can continue to evolve. It does line up with the intellectual curiosity, but you've got to have that agility and that ability to evolve as well." – Dick Johnson, CEO, Foot Locker
- "People who have learning agility, by definition, are humble and infinitely curious." – Niren Chaudhary, CEO, Panera Bread
- "I would say intellectual curiosity and being able to assimilate data, and also being very analytical in how they approach things is critical. I think about our CFO. He is almost insatiable in seeking out additional information to help create a perspective on something, really digging and finding different sources of information to validate his position." – Clayton Adams, CEO, Mascoma Savings Bank

- "The baseline is character. The second thing I look for is intellectual curiosity. People who tend to want to learn and grow. Beyond that, I obviously look at attitude. I think attitude plays so much into everything. Another key attribute is passion. Not just passion, but what they are passionate about—what motivates them and why." – Larry Schreiber, CEO, SanteFe Health Care, Inc.
- "While we have some precise leadership traits (against which we measure the performance of our leaders), when you are looking for potential, you're looking for general and intellectual curiosity. People not only have to be interested in what's going on around them but curious as to why things happen. For future leaders I am looking for intellectual curiosity, a willingness to accept the responsibility that comes with leadership and a real interest in, and care for, people." Norman Soutar, CEO, William Jackson Food Group
- Several CEOs specifically spoke about the importance of risk-taking and learning from failure as indicated in this representative comment:
  - "Take risks in a limited way and learn from them. Leaders need to learn how to take calculated risks. If things don't go as planned, there is always something there they can learn from that experience." – Chip Bergh, CEO, Levi Strauss & Co.

Adaptability (similar to results and change agility). The second most common way in which CEOs (nine) spoke of learning agility was in the realm of needing to be adaptive and stay relevant. Representative comments from CEOs are:

- "You think about 2020: none of us had a playbook for what we're facing today. We've had to put a premium on learning, agility, adaptation, and the ability to be flexible in these environments. More and more in this environment, we're also testing for that agility and learning agility. We're testing for curiosity, people who are really interested in continuing to learn." – Brian Cornell, CEO, Target
- "Recognizing reality is quite a skill because most often human beings have a lot going on in their brain and don't have true clarity or reflection." – Nachi Junankar, CEO, Avrio AI
- "Learning agility is when, quickly, someone stops focusing on things that don't matter because it would be too much energy for what's going to come out of it or because something changed in the

environment...and to redeploy those efforts to the things that they can succeed at. So, learning agility is critical to be able to succeed." – Tom O'Mara, CEO, Eligius Advisory, LLC

- "Without change, there is no transformation. It's that simple." – Keith Herman, CEO, IPA Equities
- "It is not only being able to learn that is important but also the ability to unlearn what you have learned." – Niren Chaudhary, CEO, Panera Bread
- "We need someone who is agile. Someone who adapts quickly in a broad way...how they work, where they work, etc." – Carel Nolte, CEO, CN&CO
- "Nothing is certain and if you have a leader that just wants to work in a very programmatic and predictable environment, ours are not the industries for you, and this is not the company for you. You have to be comfortable with ambiguity and being able to change direction quickly. Because we're so heavily regulated, things can change overnight, and the competition moves very fast." – Larry Schreiber, CEO, SanteFe Health Care, Inc.

Emphasis on growth every day. Seven CEOs emphasized the need to grow each day in their reflections on learning agility. Being hungry to learn, still learning every day, should want to learn every day, being proactive and learning on the go, changing direction, constantly learning are all the principles that reflect that learning should not stop.

- Bill Hewitt, CEO, Aternity, expressed it well when he offered, "To me, if you're not learning every day, I think you go stale. You then get behind; whether that's market awareness, product skills, or technical capabilities, you have to stay current. So, you have no choice if you want to deliver at a high level to constantly be learning."
- "Learning never stops. I would always tell my team that as much as you may learn from me, I learned from you. Every conversation is an opportunity." – Vineet Kumar, CEO, Intellyk, Inc.
- "People who are coachable are the best leaders." Priya Amin, CEO, Flexable

Intelligence and motivation (similar to mental agility). Several CEOs (9) indicated that they associated learning agility with two other IMPLs – motivation and intelligence, as represented in the following statement:

- "To me, learning agility sort of goes along with motivation level. Many of the skills that I have are self-taught, and I've worked in entrepreneurial companies where I've been asked to do things that I had no idea how to do them, and I just had to figure it out." – Melissa Hubbard, CEO, Kerrits Activewear, LLC

Others associated learning agility with intelligence, or "would bucket that into smart," and emphasized the capability to learn quickly.

Consequence of not learning. Five CEOs specifically spoke of the consequence of not having strong learning agility.

- Tim Kilpin, CEO, PlayMonster, reflected on whether people are "ahead of the curve or behind the curve? It's fascinating because the people who stayed behind the curve are not successful and will not be successful because the world is changing."
- "It's pretty important. On the flip side, there are plenty of people who may not have leadership potential. They like where they are, and they're excellent and confident in what they do. In those cases, their agility may not necessarily be a high priority. It's just that if the company pivots, they're usually eliminated." – Sharad Joshi, CEO, Satio, Inc.

How to Assess Learning Agility?

Surprisingly, because of how important it seems to be, not many CEOs mentioned using tools such as assessments, case studies, or tests. Most responses in the CEO study related to observation in one form or another – language, application, performance, and curiosity.

Observing – language. Many CEOs spoke of observing learning agility. There were several elements these CEOs were observing.

- One such element was in the language used. "If you can tell they're here to come in and just, oh, I've got this mindset and ethos, and I'm going to dictate that on to this new environment and they're not here to learn, they're here to command and demand. That's not a learning mindset. That's just going to create more chaos." – Samir Patel, CEO, Moonlight Therapeutics, Inc.
- Other CEOs indicated they assess this through questioning in the interview process. Sample questions included, "Do you have a broad

range? Do you have a framework within which you operate? Or do you only know about people that look and sound like you? Do you only read on a particular topic?" – Carel Nolte, CEO, CN&CO

- Another CEO mentioned using presentations and case studies during the interview process and observe how they handled this CEOs questions in that forum. "When we hire people, we put them through a series of case studies that determine how they think." – Jane Page, CEO, Lionstone Investments
- Julia Stewart, founder and CEO at Alurx, places an importance not just upon a candidate's answers, but how they arrive at their answers. "It is important for her to see an agility in the candidates' responses. And if those responses are supported with an element of storytelling – that's a big plus. Conversely, if there is a question that is off-putting or simply stumps them altogether, that's a red flag."

Observing – application. Other modes of observing were in how they applied the knowledge they learned. Alison Croke, CEO, Wood River Health Services, indicated, "If they are not capable of change, it shows up pretty quickly in this environment." Another example of this sentiment was from Coco Brown, CEO, The Athena Alliance, "You want people to say, 'When this happened, Coco, you shared it with me, and I took it to heart, and here is what I've done as a result.' Not have them say, 'Yeah, I know you said that before' without any indication of internalization or indication they have or intend to incorporate the feedback as learning."

Observing – performance. Several CEOs noted that it is best observed through the work they do and their performance, such as assessing their work through projects. Others mentioned seeking whether they take risks and whether they are curious. Do they problem-solve, collaborate?

Jyoti Gupta, CEO, Volk Optical, speaks of creating opportunities to see how they perform.

> I've often had candidates do presentations centered around complex problems they have personally solved. It is open-ended and they can choose their own scenarios and topics from their own experiences. Having them present helps me see how they structure their thoughts and how well they understand the problem they solved. Digging into the presentation helps me get clarity regarding what they have done and why. What I'm trying to figure out is if they actually did the work or were simply around other people who did the work. Someone who truly did the work will be able to go into excruciating detail about the issues at hand, why certain

decisions were made and why those decisions were sound at the time. Those who are intellectually curious will appreciate probing and challenging questions and engage in meaningful dialogue/debate versus others who may get defensive or agitated. I use these case studies and presentations as a way to probe and challenge to see how people think, how and why they make decisions, and how they respond to questions that may sometimes challenge their work – this gives me some indication of how they will perform in the role: can they handle tough questions, do they understand and solve problems fundamentally, how might they react if certain aspects of the scenarios they presented change, can they think on their feet and can they operate in the face of uncertainty? It also gives me an idea of their ability to structure and communicate their thoughts to an audience who may know nothing about the topic and their ability to connect the dots and think at a systemic level.

Observing – curiosity. Several (4) CEOs indicated they use demonstrated curiosity as a method to assess learning agility.

- "I assess it by getting some senses of how curious people are about things. Who is it that goes out and is a self-directed, self-guided learner?" – Jandel T. Allen-Davis, CEO, Craig Hospital
- "Learning agility looks like those who are curious and ask questions about our business strategy, our go-to-market strategy, and our product development process. Are they curious? Are they asking good questions? Are they digging deep to figure out what things mean and how they relate and can be effective?" – Bill Hewitt, CEO, Aternity
- "I track very closely the people that have decided to go off and [pursue interests] such as taking a coding course or a different approach to leadership style or adapting their own style." – Bill Winters, CEO, Standard Charter Bank
- "What are they learning, and how are they learning? How much is an individual reading? Do they follow their industry or aware of the broader business environment? It's not just about what an individual takes in, it's just as important they think about its application." – John Lawlor, CEO, Maugel Architects.

Good News – It's Developable!

Unlike intelligence but similar to motivation, learning agility is developable. Ironically, learning agility can be learned (Hallenbeck, 2016).

It takes grit, discipline, focus, and a systematic approach from some-one who is persistent and committed to increasing their capacity to accomplish it. Changing behavior is not easy. One study tested learn-ing agility at the beginning of a program and then at the end. The five components of learning agility were assessed, and each component increased by at least ten percentile points (some had increased dou-ble that amount) over the three-year span of the program (Buckner & Marberry, 2018). Another study conducted at the Center for Creative Leadership showed improved learning agility in a program that ran one day a month with homework between learning events (Eichinger, 2018).

It is more easily developable when you are wired that way to start. Approximately 15% of employees have high learning agility (Knight & Wong, 2020). Learning agility comes partly from neurology result-ing from people who are more naturally agile in learning, being quick, and able to change (Harvey & De Meuse, 2021) and partly from per-sonality. However, as indicated through these numerous studies, it is developable, and a company constructively fostering a learning culture can enable more success by having employees increase their learning agility.

Summary and Recommended Path Forward

Learning agility is widely agreed upon as a difference maker in accu-rately determining leadership potential. The ability to continually reinvent yourself to be current and add value is a tremendous com-petitive advantage for the companies who employ such people. It is simply critical for today's leaders to have a high learning agility. Each of the five components of learning agility – mental, people, change, results, and self-awareness – needs to be more fully understood. This is a fairly straightforward, non-controversial, reliable, and predictable indicator of potential. What's curious is we are not overtly sourcing for and discussing it more robustly. People show us their learning agility in the interview process based on their preparation for the interview. If someone doesn't research me before I interview them...they are out. It's a simple test, hard to fail, easy to pass. If they cannot take the three minutes to be better informed about a conversation – they don't belong with us.

If you are truly serious, start with these steps:

1. Read up on learning agility. There is much written today that can help you become proficient in understanding and leveraging it.
2. Curiosity and adaptability are close cousins of learning agility. Try to weave these concepts into the conversation and see what traction you get.
3. There are good assessments for learning agility. Take one yourself and see what you learn. Use that to experiment with your team and see what it tells you. Going forward, figure out how to incorporate it into your assessment process for internal and external candidates.
4. Pay attention to people's language. So much of learning agility is revealed through language.
5. Ambition is a good thing. Ambition that blinds someone to the impact they have on others or prevents them from being realistic about their skillsets and areas of development are derailers. But treat ambition with kindness and capitalize on it. High performers with high learning agility are almost always high potentials. Don't let another employer tell them in an interview process how much they appreciate their ambition. Make sure you are honing it and not stuck with arbitrary indicators of success like tenure.
6. Have high standards. People don't need to have countless advanced degrees, but they need to continually seek, absorb, evolve, and be a better version of themselves.
7. Check out determiningleadershippotential.com for a great list of sample interview/assessment questions.

Visit **determiningleadershippotential.com** for case studies and additional resources.

Reference List

Buckner, M., & Marberry, M. (2018). How to identify and grow high potentials: A CEO's perspective with proven results. *People & Strategy*, *41*(1), 22–28.

Eichinger, R. W. (2018). The war for how to do talent management or is there really anything new? *People & Strategy*, *41*(1), 9–12. https://link.gale.com/apps/doc/A525002296/AONE?u=anon~1002e5ae&sid=googleScholar&xid=ee20604f

Ellis, R. K. (2021, June 15). Navigate the future with learning agility. Association for Talent

Development. www.td.org/magazines/ctdo-magazine/navigate-the-future-with-learning-agility

De Meuse, K. P. (2019). *A meta-analysis of the relationship between learning agility and leader success.* Journal of Organizational Psychology.

Finkelstein, L. M., Costanza, D. P., & Goodwin, G. F. (2018). Do your high potentials have potential? The impact of individual differences and designation on leader success. *Personnel Psychology, 71*(1), 3–22.

Hallenbeck, G. (2016). *Learning agility: Unlock the lessons of experience.* Center for Creative Leadership, Greensboro, NC.

Harvey, V. S., & De Meuse, K. P. (2021). *The age of agility: Developing agile leaders and organizations.* Oxford University Press, New York.

Knight, M., & Wong, N. (2020, October 21). The organisational X-factor: Learning agility. Korn Ferry Focus. https://focus.kornferry.com/leadership-and-talent/the-organisational-x-factor-learning-agility/

Lasse, C. (2020, September 1). Pivot and adapt. Association for Talent Development. www.td.org/magazines/td-magazine/pivot-and-adapt

10

Assessments and Tools

Kimberly Janson and Melody Rawlings

One of the most underutilized strategies in determining leadership potential is the use of tools and assessments to better inform our decision-making. However, when asked what would help people in this area, understanding and use of tools and assessments rose to the top of the ideas offered. This is particularly important because most people who are "observing" are not trained observers, yet observation was cited 90+% of the time as the chief mechanism being used to assess each of the IMPLs. Think about it this way. We all can watch a quarterback throw a football and have an opinion about it. Still, someone who knows what to look for in angle of the arm, foot stance, where the eyes are trained, etc., will better understand the nuances and assess the competence of quarterbacks than you or I. Just like any important skill to perfect, detecting these four vital components (intelligence, personality, motivation, and learning agility) should come with specialized training to enable success. This chapter delivers strong insight from CEOs on the use of assessments to bridge the gap between what they do and what they want as well as a list of available assessments and the authors' recommendations.

In the global quantitative study, we asked participants what assistance they would like to be more successful in this work, and the result was nearly 50 comments on assessments. Leaders want effective data and objective assessments. They want appropriate assessments for the work. They want to be trained in how to use them and understand what they do. Specific assessments that surfaced throughout this study were:

- 58% use 360-degree feedback tools
- 50% use Myers–Briggs
- 41% use DiSC

DOI: 10.4324/9781003272212-10

- 10% use an IQ assessment
- 7% use Watson Glaser.

CEOs also had a strong point of view about wanting to use assessments better and more often.

- "We do a lot of testing. I know my weaknesses, and I want to cover them with people who can do what I can't do…I choose to surround myself with those who perform well in my areas of weakness." – Michael Levy, CEO, Crow Holdings
- "We would use psychometric profiling for leadership development to help individuals understand themselves more than anything else." – Norman Soutar, CEO, William Jackson Food Group
- "We manage as a team, and we develop as a team. Everybody in the executive suite comes together, and we go through everybody at the director and above level and normalize across that. It's about 60 individuals that fill in the director, VP roles, officer roles, and we talked to each of those individuals as a group, and the ones that kind of float up the top are the ones who get the most attention. Then the individual C-level executives are responsible for developing a plan for that individual with them, and then we can chip away at it that way." – Trey Sutten, CEO, Cardinal Innovations Healthcare
- "Do I look at personality traits? Yes. Do I see that people demonstrate them? Yes. Do I think that sometimes those tests can be wrong? Not often. Sooner or later, whatever that assessment said was going to happen will show up. Then you get to decide whether or not that's a risk you want to take. Is it a big enough challenge for you?" – Michael Levy, CEO, Crow Holdings.

Ken Hicks, CEO, Academy Sports & Outdoors, provided a good example of using multiple assessments:

> At some of the companies I worked at we would give people a battery of tests. Some were the IQ test, and some were leadership. They're helpful and usually are indicative. They aren't descriptive, but they're indicative. I think you learn a person's ability by watching the person, seeing how they operate and the decisions they make and the way they process data and situations.

Christelle Colman, CEO, Elite Risk Acceptances, spoke of a critical point – trusting the data and the process. She also shares a unique technique called speed interviewing,

Our company is part of a bigger corporation, so we have everything at our disposal, and we do use it. In the most recent interviews, we used something called speed interviewing. We actually had internally about 150 people applied for the role. We conducted the psychometric testing, the aptitude testing, and the interview. We rely on the data and trust the process.

A sampling of comments indicating what leaders are looking for included:

- "We spend significant time on identification...perhaps a new tool to help do that more efficiently and accurately."
- "Providing more tools that have proven effectiveness."
- "Better support from HR with executing the employee development plans."
- "In addition to greater self-identification, I would like to see us do better at consistent tools, diversity, and consistent cross-leader assessment. Too often, leaders pick candidates who look/act like them."
- "Explaining the suitable tool for me to determine a successful leader."
- "Specific valid tools."
- "Our company needs to better its tools and ability to determine leadership potential. The newer tools need to be introduced and utilized rather than older ones that don't always work in today's world."
- "The opportunity to use testing services to help better pinpoint the strengths and weaknesses of key leaders."
- "Better tools."
- "It's always such a qualitative assessment, right? It would be helpful if a company quantified the process somehow and everyone knew where they stood."
- "More tools, emphasis, and rewards to the manager who has a team member promoted, the company focus on promoting from within, uncovering talents within."

There are several considerations when selecting a tool:

- Quality – what is the quality of the output, readability, complexity, and usefulness?
- Reliability – how dependable and consistent are the results? Can the test be manipulated?
- Validity – is the assessment method useful for predicting outcomes?

- Adverse impact – do members of protected groups systematically score lower than others?
- Time – how long do the assessments take and what amount of time needs to be invested in understanding them?
- Cost – what is the expense of developing, administering, and maintaining the assessment?
- Candidate reaction – do candidates react positively or negatively to the assessment?
- Raters – do you want a self-assessment, or do you want to include key stakeholders such as managers, external experts, or all the above in the process?

Types of Assessments

Once an organization has bought into the idea and value of using assessments, the next big question is where to start. There are more than 2,500 assessments in the market today, just for personality alone (Church & Ezama, 2020)! This can create a great deal of confusion in the market on what to use and when. Organizations are teaching managers how to use such tools and hiring external experts to assist with the instruments' choice, quality, and accuracy.

Sample assessments can fall into these categories:

- 360
- Competency measures
- Cognitive tests
- Personality inventories
- Learning agility
- Structured behavioral interviews
- Simulations
- Case studies
- Or a combined method assessing multiple traits with multiple methods (MTMM).

With so much on the market and our deep belief that assessments are critical to effectively determining potential, we have dedicated the rest of this chapter to giving you a brief primer on the more common assessments. This is not an exhaustive list, and we are not experts in each of these tools but are experts in some of them. It's important to agree there is simply no perfect assessment...yet. This list is intended to facilitate your thinking to help you determine where you should put further effort into research to understand your options more fully. We've divided this list into two groupings. The first part is our preferred set of instruments, and the second is a listing of other instruments commonly used.

Our Preferred Instruments Arranged Alpha Order

360-degree instruments. This tool allows multiple raters that surround the employee (360 view of the employee) to provide perspective on specific attributes. It is the most commonly used tool (Church et al., 2015). A popular one is Survey Sparrow's 360, but our preferred one is DecisionWise. They have a standard 360, but for a reasonable price point they will create a custom 360 to fit your organization. Time to complete varies based on the number of questions in the assessment and whether the answer choices are along a Likert scale or open-ended requiring a written answer.

DiSC. A simple but informative, very popular tool that Kim has used for more than 25 years. It uses a scale to assess degrees of dominance, influence, steadiness, and conscientiousness. Provides a high-level understanding of preferences. DiSC is easy to use, easy to administer, and takes approximately 10–15 minutes to complete.

Hogan. This instrument is one of our favorites because of its comprehensiveness and usefulness. It is intended to predict job success and is widely used for high-potential assessment and executive development. It is one of or the most commonly used executive assessments globally. It is used by at least 75% of the Fortune 500 companies. There are three components to the suite of assessments.

- MVPI – Motives, Values, Preferences Inventory
- HPI – Hogan Personality Inventory
- HDS – Hogan Development Survey.

Learning Agility

As we have documented, learning agility is one of the most reliable predictors of potential. The first formal assessment, the Choices Architect, measures four agilities: mental, people, change, and results. It was developed by Lombardo and Eichinger and built upon by the Center of Creative Leadership (Hoff & Burke, 2017). All current assessments have been built upon this original work, which is still available.

We prefer two sets of learning agility assessments. One set is offered through Korn Ferry. They have positioned themselves as experts in assessing learning agility.

- Choices Architect is a multi-rater questionnaire that measures the four agilities.
- viaEDGE is a self-reporting instrument that measures four agilities plus self-awareness.
- LFE, learning from experience, is a structured interview approach focusing on four agilities.
- They also have a learning agility simulation that measures participants' observing, connecting, and assessing abilities while completing online exercises and simulations.

Burke LAI. The other preferred instrument is the Burke LAI, which measures flexibility and speed. Flexibility emphasizes abandoning the behaviors that worked in the past for new, more successful behaviors. It involves both unlearning and learning. Speed measures how quickly an individual can pivot, read situations, and form a plan of action. There are different assessments for selection and development, including one for multi-rater assessment, which is Burke360LAS.

Both assessments require trained professionals to implement and utilize the instruments. There are others, such as TALENTx7 and Aon Hewitt/Kincentric's Accelerated Learning Model. All four measure cognitive, social, and self, as well as motivation, ability, and application (Harvey & De Meuse, 2021). They are four strong instruments to measure learning agility, with our preference being the first two.

Myers–Briggs Type Indicator (MBTI). This instrument is based on Carl Jung's theories and has been used for more than 50 years. It is complex and delves into character traits to identify 16 personality types. Their four scales include extrovert vs. introvert, thinking vs. feeling, judging vs. perceiving, and sensing vs. intuition.

Power of Understanding People. This assessment is like DiSC but is even quicker and it is free in the author's book by the same title. Through the assessment, and his book, Dave Mitchell provides a fun and interactive way to better understand self and others to produce better results.

Wonderlic. This assessment measures cognitive ability. Through 50 questions that must be answered in 12 minutes, participants answer questions relating to simple math, basic logic, language comprehension, spatial reasoning, pattern identification, and more that become increasingly difficult to answer as the test progresses.

Our Preferred Approach

We found that we can most accurately predict potential when using a combination of tools to assess and develop high potentials. Our preference is to use a custom 360-degree instrument for internal candidates that encapsulates the priority behaviors and competencies specifically for that organization. We call this the outside-in perspective. We then will combine that with the Hogan Assessment – all three components, the DiSC for behavioral preferences understanding, the Wonderlic for cognitive assessment, and one of the learning agility assessments mentioned above. The approach above is a multi-trait, multi-method (MTMM) approach, similar to the PepsiCo approach but not nearly as customized or comprehensive. The suggested approach above provides a robust evaluation for future executive success and development (Buckner & Marberry, 2018).

The CEO of Levi Strauss & Co, Chip Bergh, shared his MTMM approach:

> I use a consulting firm called RHR who are all psychologists to conduct executive assessments. I went through these deep assessments conducted by psychologists myself. Based on the assessment, we create a development plan for each executive. I also use a 360 for each of my direct reports. We use Hogan, a quantitative test, 3-hour interviews with PhD psychologist, outside blind assessment of their resume and then stack them up against our readiness stack.

Validity

Based on your needs, be sure to structure an approach based on a consistently applied, reliable, and legally defendable set of assessments (Church & Rotolo, 2013). It is important to use instruments validated by the assessment creator/vendor, but you need to validate them for your own company (Church & Ezama, 2020). This consists of having a pilot phase, thoroughly analyzing the results, not just individually, but across the set of participants, which is critical to determining trends and potential biases. Be sure to look for adverse impacts and ensure your selection processes and tools do not harm specific groups of people regarding race, sex, religion, age, disability, and veteran status.

If you are unsure as to how to go about this work, engage an industrial-organizational (I-O) psychologist for help. One example of this was provided by David Hurwitz, CEO Transaction Capital. "We have a small local business we use, and all of our employees have psychometric testing. We have internal and external coaches." This is a great example of combining knowledge of the company with knowledge of instruments and approaches that need to be used properly.

Summary and Recommended Path Forward

The bottom line of this chapter is that tools and assessments work. They add more data and a little science to our assessment work. We have been mightily uninformed and, in some cases, we have been lazy in this space. This is a simple area to improve and more fully leverage. There are tremendous resources to help and a wide array of tools to use. Be informed, however, on the limitations of any tool you use and work to make sure it is defendable. If you are not able to make such judgements, leverage literature and expertise to help.

If you are truly serious, start with these steps:

1. Identify five new instruments and try them to see what information they provide and how you can use them. Continue to experiment and whittle it to the ones that work best to tell you information about the critical indicators of potential.
2. Identify a subject matter expert you can leverage for advice and counsel on instruments.
3. Ask people their favorite approach – tool or assessment – and determine why.
4. Look to leverage a multi-trait, multi-method approach.
5. It is hard to replace multi-rater feedback that helps you understand how people are experiencing you, so make sure a 360 is part of your data collection.

6. Simulations and case studies are simply under-used. Be a pace-setter and create some that can help you source candidates' thinking and ways of working.
7. Don't be afraid of assessments. They can be intimidating if you have not used a particular one. Apply your high learning agility and make a list of ones that seem to have appeal. Try to learn about one every other week and in no time, you will have increased your knowledge base and list of options.

Visit **determiningleadershippotential.com** for case studies and additional resources.

Reference List

Buckner, M., & Marberry, M. (2018). How to identify and grow high potentials: A CEO's perspective with proven results. *People & Strategy*, *41*(1), 22–28.

Church, A., & Ezama, S. (2020, April 1). PepsiCo's formula for leadership potential. Association for Talent Development. www.td.org/magazines/td -magazine/pepsicos-formula-for-leadership-potential

Church, A. H., & Rotolo, C. T. (2013). How are top companies assessing their high-potentials and senior executives? A talent management benchmark study. *Consulting Psychology Journal: Practice and Research*, *65*(3), 199–223.

Church, A. H., Rotolo, C. T., Ginther, N. M., & Levine, R. (2015). How are top companies designing and managing their high-potential programs? A follow-up talent management benchmark study. *Consulting Psychology Journal: Practice and Research*, *67*(1), 17–47.

Harvey, V. S., & De Meuse, K. P. (2021). *The age of agility: Developing agile leaders and organizations*. Oxford University Press, New York.

Hoff, D. F., & Burke, W. W. (2017). *Learning agility: The key to leader potential*. Hogan Press, Tulsa, OK.

11

Wrapping It Up and Putting Ideas into Action

Kimberly Janson and Melody Rawlings

Let's finish strong! We have the opportunity to create a legacy and become wildly successful at determining leadership potential, and getting this right is crucial for everyone! This chapter summarizes and highlights key takeaways from chapters 1–10 and offers recommendations with actionable steps toward improving how we determine leadership potential in others. While this chapter provides a quick summary, more importantly, it offers a robust send-off with clear next steps, a quick reference tool for using the Leadership Blueprint, a pledge to get on track, and an invitation to stay connected through the link provided at the end of the chapter.

First, here are some of the highlights of the road we travelled:

- We've fully explored the significance of poor leadership and why getting it right at the start is the best way to combat this issue
- We've done a deep dive into a relatable and extremely useful framework – the Leadership Blueprint
- We came to understand, through a meta-analysis of the DLP research and through three of our own research studies, how people are thinking about DLP and the major issues that make us less effective
- We more fully understand the concept and importance of intelligence in DLP as well as how to think about it and assess it
- We've delved into the complicated components of personality and are particularly vigilant about dark traits and the vital nature of emotional intelligence
- We've gotten a good handle on both learning agility and motivation including their importance, what they look like, and how to assess them
- We have explored a boatload of assessments and tools

DOI: 10.4324/9781003272212-11

Many CEOs shared the great success they have had in doing this work. "There are 33 people who have worked for me through the years who have become CEOs themselves. I'm pretty proud of that. Chip Bergh, CEO, Levi Strauss & Co. That's unbelievable!

Ken Hicks, CEO, Academy Sports + Outdoors, who was CEO of seven companies, shared how much it meant that people recognized his building of strong leaders and teams.

> Allen leaned over to me, and he said, you know, this is the best operations team I think I've ever had the privilege of working with. When I was at Foot Locker, after about four years, we were having a board dinner with my executive team and the lead director leaned over to me, and he said, "You assembled a great team here."

These CEOs have created a pace for us in this work. A textbook case of who has done this well is Allan Church at PepsiCo.

A Case Study in Doing it Right

The Gold Standard Example – Allan Church and PepsiCo

Having studied many companies, we see PepsiCo as the leader of their process and outcomes in determining leadership potential. The work at PepsiCo is led by a brilliant practitioner – Allan Church. Kim had the opportunity to spend a great deal of time with Allan in the context of understanding the Leadership Blueprint, and he generously shared his time and insights. Allan is one of the co-founders of the Leadership Blueprint. Allan has built a talent machine over the last eight years that produced reliable and repeatable results culminating in a strong pipeline of leaders.

PepsiCo – a multi-billion-dollar global consumer package goods company – uses a custom integrated system to enable reliable high-potential assessment and development. Their program – leadership assessment and development program – called LEAD, has assessed over ten thousand leaders, including most senior leaders. It uses an MTMM approach that synthesizes leadership potential into an assessment index. Details of the index, based on a predictive algorithm and how candidates score against the assessment, are shared with employees. PepsiCo uses a combination of 360s, cognitive tests, personality measures, customized business simulations, and a competency model called GREAT 5 (growth, relationships, execution, agility, thinking). In addition, they have focused on creating high validity year after year. PepsiCo completely sponsors the entire process. Without a doubt, the work Allan Church has done at PepsiCo is the pace-setter for all other organizations.

As illustrated by Allan's work, having professionals with deep subject matter expertise is critical yet missing in most organizations. HR needs to become stronger and much more of an asset to the business in this space. HR practitioners and talent management professionals must influence managers concerning how to choose employees with the potential to be strong leaders (Reynolds et al., 2018). Most HR professionals (82%) view their organizations as strong in this area or believe that their leader bench is strong enough to effectively address the needs of future business performance (DDI, 2018). Frankly, they are wrong, and most are not qualified to make those assessments. If they were, perhaps we would not have the leadership crisis we have today.

Our Best Advice

We asked people in our global quantitative study and the CEO study what hinders you in this work, the significant challenges you face, and what would help. Finally, we folded in our own experiences, and below, in summary, is our best advice on how to completely raise your game in this area and where to go from here.

1. COMMIT

Lack of authentic leader commitment from those responsible for this work is one of the most significant root causes of our many issues surrounding the determination of leadership potential. Commitment comes most frequently in the area of time.

When we asked leaders their biggest challenge, the biggest hindrance, or what would help – the universal answer was: time. We heard them say it is hard to find time, that there is so much in the day-to-day, we need to deal with crises, etc. So, here's our clinical response to time being an issue: buck up, buttercup. We have the time. We are just not prioritizing this work above other things, or we need to be more efficient in working or underutilizing the talent around us.

Without fail, we see this with great clarity as we go into organizations. Remember Steven Covey's *7 Habits of Highly Successful People* and the urgent vs. the important concept? It's alive and well as a current problem in organizations. Own this. It's like when people say – I don't have time to read a book…everyone can read 10 minutes a day or 10 pages a day. Or…I don't have time to exercise – everyone has 20 minutes a day to walk. Do not accept this as an excuse from yourself or others. Plan the work and then work the plan so that over time, you have a robust set of management routines that are integrated into how you run your business. Don't be lulled into only spending time on the tangibles because, before you know it, you will have talent and leadership issues showing up in very tangible ways.

The other factor about time is that leaders will say they want this stuff but then abandon ship because it takes time. We have direct experience with leadership teams not wanting to put in the time to get the results back on assessments. Instead, they want to interview and decide *fast*. They say they want to do assessments but don't like all that it comes with – so it all gets canned. And speaking of getting canned…the result of these behaviors is that organizations let people go within a year. This is directly why bad decisions are made – talking out of both sides of our mouths, moving too fast, and not having the patience to let the process work. We are so frustrated when senior leaders engage in magical thinking about time but expect different results. Let's be honest with ourselves and be better.

To do this work well, a smaller investment of effort over a specific amount of time is the best approach to observe a range of behaviors, underlying values, and sourcing for the items we called out in the Leadership Blueprint. This is short-cycled when hiring from the outside. Even for outside hires, however, we should put as much of a diligent process together as we can for external candidates…as similar to what we create for internal candidates. We live in a soundbite world, so work to get a broader view of people.

Robin van Rozen, CEO, Glen Dimplex, reminds us of the criticality of committing and putting in the time.

I think first is to create the time to have the discussions. I don't think you can do the process justice in isolation. It is not something I can do on my own determining. You need a team effort where you discuss people and assess if somebody is to the finish or not on the criteria of like before. So, my wish list is always creating room as we have recent conversations.

Michael Levy, CEO, Crow Holdings, shares a story where it was challenging for him to focus on these priorities earlier in his career. However, with that said, he still emphasized the need for time in this work.

Time. These things take time. At Morgan Stanley, in my last five years at the firm, I worked in multiple groups with different jobs and multiple bosses. They kept throwing at me in the first few months, "What could you do to fix what's broken?" So, I never had time to step back and think, work with people, develop trust, take my time, and be thoughtful. But it's all about people.

Make this work *the* priority because everything else cascades from having the right talent.

2. USE LEADERSHIP BLUEPRINT (OR A DEFINED FRAMEWORK/PROCESS)

Many people asked for a way to look at this work in a concerted, more analytical, more concrete way. They asked for a lens to focus questions and understand what characteristics to look for in their quest.

People are begging for more structure around this. Give them a process and hold yourself and the organization to it.

1. **Agree on the framework.** Ensure everyone is educated on what it is and how to use it.
2. **Use common definitions.** Have a shared definition of leadership potential, the criteria you will use, a definition for high potentials, and ensure *everyone* is on the same page on these items.
3. **Implement a talent planning process.** Kim runs a talent planning process with many of her clients that takes a unique look at talent, fueled by data and assessments, and creates a forum for the senior leaders in the company to converge regularly to talk about talent. It works.

4. **Define and use metrics.** Determine metrics for success. Senior leaders want to quantify results, which will make your business cause more compelling or inform you of adjustments that need to be made.

Leadership Blueprint Cheat Sheet

Consult each chapter for a more thorough set of recommendations.

1. **Assess against the Foundational Dimension** – Personality and Intelligence
   - Assess for intelligence – use great interview questions, create scenarios to test candidates, use the Wonderlic Assessment.
   - Assess for personality – use the DiSC to understand behavioral preferences and Hogan Personality Inventory (HPI) and Hogan Development Survey (HDS...for derailers or dark traits), spend time with candidates in various situations to learn about them, use great interview questions.

   Decision – Did they pass each of these thresholds? If yes, continue. If not, be courageous and recognize they do not have the necessary components to be a strong leader. If yes, assess their learning agility and motivation.
2. **Assess against the Growth Dimension** – Motivation and Learning Agility
   - Assess motivation – use the Hogan Motives, Values, Preferences Inventory (MVPI), and spend time to truly understand what is essential to the candidates. Then, put them in scenarios over time to develop a reliable point of view.
   - Assess learning agility – use Choice Architect or viaEDGE. Put them in scenarios over time to develop a reliable point of view. Then, test them and watch for the five components of learning agility.

   Decision – Did they pass each of these thresholds? If yes, continue. If not, be courageous and recognize they do not have the necessary components to be a strong leader. If they did, assess their current leadership capabilities and, if necessary, their functional abilities.

   Remember – behavior always trumps what the assessments say, but the assessments are generally correct, so dig under what you see to truly understand it.

3. **Assess against the Career Dimension** – Leadership Capabilities and Technical Skills

   The premise behind this dimension is an individual has the previous four components, and we can teach them leadership and technical skills. That means that we have determined they indeed have a deep passion for being a leader and for investing in their capabilities over time.

   1. **Leadership capabilities** – have a defined leadership model that you use for your company that identifies the most important leadership capabilities needed. There are off-the-shelf products you could use, but a custom one isn't difficult to have created and is much more powerful. Use a 360 to assess current performance against these desired capabilities.

   2. **Functional capabilities** – use functional competency models and well-crafted functional interview questions to assess competence. A multi-rater perspective is also helpful in creating specific "tests – simulations, case studies, scenarios" to help inform your point of view. Functional associations (ex. AAA – American Accounting Association) often have functional competency models you can leverage.

Whatever the gap, it is developable and should be done through a specific development plan for each individual that is agreed upon, tracked, and adjusted as needed.

All of this work gets compounded when hiring from the outside. When asked what would help to determine leadership potential when hiring from the outside, Larry Schreiber, CEO, SanteFe Health Care, Inc., provided this great advice.

> Truth serum! But seriously, as you're recruiting from the outside and assessing leadership, some people talk a really good game. The resume looks good, they talk good, and the references *they* provide will always check out. That's where having a team approach to interviewing is an incredibly powerful tool. Having a diverse team getting eyes on somebody can provide you with a 360-degree view of a person's strengths and opportunities for development. In addition, you have to dig deeper than their references, who were hand-picked and often coached by the candidate in advance. In today's hyper-connected world, it's easy to connect with informal references. I've found that in business, it's not six degrees of separation. It tends to be two degrees, or even one. It just takes a little extra time and effort to ferret out those individuals that look good and talk good but have some challenges in their past.

Don't abandon your commitment to being thorough and diligent because it is an external candidate. All of this advice becomes even more important at that point!

3. GET COMPETENT IN MAKING TOUGH DECISIONS AND HAVING TOUGH CONVERSATIONS

No doubt that it can be difficult to make tough decisions about people. But that's your job. If you don't want to do it, return the paycheck, and find an alternative. It's the job. To help remember the stark realities of tough conversations, here are some tenets you must subscribe to if you are going to be effective in this work and produce strong leaders:

- Not everyone is going to be a leader.
- People require and deserve transparency, even if it is not what they want to hear.
- Radical candor is difficult but denying people the opportunity to misunderstand is the kinder thing for them than ignoring the issue.
- Having tough conversations is an improved skill with knowledge and practice.
- People have made choices about their careers. How hard they have worked on themselves, etc. These are not your choices. You are not destroying lives by deciding someone is not a fit. Being highly employable is their responsibility.
- God or nature (or whomever you believe in) gave people their intelligence and personality. Who are we to think we can change those? Be honest with yourself.
- You can be tough-minded while still respectful, kind, and caring. Help people land well in alternative jobs and situations whenever you can. This does not mean passing a problem to someone else.
- This is never better the longer it takes. These issues do not age well. Be efficient in your decision-making. (We have never heard a leader say, "Oh, I wish I took *more* time before making that decision about that person.")
- Inconsistent performers, the C+ and B– types with moments of brilliance and failure are not worth your time. Instead, learn what it is like to have an A-player team of leaders and not settle.
- Evolving companies sometimes outgrow their leaders.
- Match potential with ambition. Don't kid yourself on either factor.

- Remove blockers. This one is additionally difficult because those people are likely "fine." But certain roles are critical for the development of others and should not be occupied by people who have no upward mobility, aka blockers.
- People can be excellent performers in their current roles and maximize their potential.
- Yes, firing, demoting, or moving people in ways they don't want just plainly stinks. There is no way around that. It just does.

Pledge an oath here and now:

> I, _____, will not hide from people issues. I will not push them under the rug because I don't want to make people feel bad. I will not fail my company or team members by being irresponsible in this area. It is my job to act. I was put into a role to make tough decisions that are important for the organization's overall health. If I am not good at these conversations, I will get help to improve.

One last comment on this topic, ongoing feedback is not optional; it is required. This has become even more tricky because people have a variety of reactions to feedback. Larry Schreiber, CEO, SanteFe HealthCare, Inc., shared that sentiment with this insight:

> I think our current society doesn't want us to be critical. We need to embrace constructive criticism, but all too often, it is viewed as a de-motivator. Feedback is a gift. I try to balance positive feedback with input on developmental opportunities. For example, "Overall, you did a great job, *but* let's consider what could have gone better." Too often, people don't listen to anything ahead of the "*but*." The message they receive is that what I did well doesn't matter because you're going to tell me what I did wrong. That's a hindrance that needs to be overcome by hiring the right people and developing a culture where it is OK to make mistakes, as long as you learn from them.

4. INVEST IN THE DEVELOPMENT OF YOUR LEADERS

Determining leadership potential is a big idea. Getting it right is essential. We've dedicated a whole book to the concept. When you get it right, you still need to develop your leaders. Here are some truths about developing leaders:

- We cannot defy the laws of physics or gravity or the laws of development. It doesn't happen through osmosis. You need to do things to develop. People need to be taught (in some way, and there are several ways) to learn.
- And it takes time, money, and effort. If it were fast, cheap, or easy, everyone would be great leaders. Invest because it works. Training programs, books, stretch assignments, discussions, etc., are all viable ways people accumulate knowledge and skills to help them do their current or future job better.
- Coaching works. Ensure you are coaching your coaches, and make sure your people get coaching. This one is a bankable development strategy.
- Put people in as many situations as you can over time. Be intentional about it. Through various experiences that are then evaluated and re-applied, judgement is formed. Start early, be vigilant, and keep the course of developing people over time.

5. JUST BE BETTER

Keep working on being the best version of yourself in this space. Take the time to develop. Here are three areas, in particular, we implore you to address:

1. Bias. Many of our CEOs expressed concern that their own unconscious bias played into determining leadership potential. Do good work to keep surfacing your personal biases and manage by facts. This is particularly true if you are working with people who are close, loyal, and/or friends. It's also human nature to pick someone similar to you. Self-awareness is critical, and if this is difficult for you, then surround yourself with people who will help you understand and make it safe for them to discuss potential biases. As we get older, we become more deep-seated in our thinking, so be prudent about the surety of our thoughts.
2. Hone your craft with others. Find a forum to network with on ideas. Identify groups of people who are like-minded discussing these issues. Actively benchmark where others have made progress or had success.
3. Solicit folks outside your organization to be a mentor or get a coach. They are difference makers.

4. Keep your toolkit current. Do you have a great set of interview questions? Are you proficient in assessments? Do you have great examples to reference in your discussions and storytelling with the organization? Do you have well-crafted case studies to use to assess people's thinking? Make sure the equity in your toolkit keeps increasing as your 401(k) does!

5. Read. Reading is one of the biggest enablers of executive success. Set small and specific reading goals and fulfill them.

6. Stay in touch with us. We will continue to be a purveyor of thought leaders in this area. Subscribe to our blog and read our articles. Complete our self-assessment tool on the website to help you evaluate how well you determine leadership potential in others. Visit our website (determiningleadershippotential.com or jansonassociates. com) for stories to access, case studies to use, and other resources we will be offering in an ongoing manner.

In closing, we would like to thank you for taking the time to make yourself better by reading this book. The world will be better for it.

Visit **determiningleadershippotential.com** for case studies and many more resources to help you on this journey of solving this world crisis and making you even more effective at determining leadership potential.

Reference List

DDI (2018). *Five best practices of identifying potential leaders.* www.oracle. com/us/products/applications/talent-mgmt-potenital-leaders-2095829.pdf

Reynolds, D. H., McCauley, C. D., & Tsacoumis, S. (2018). A critical evaluation of the state of assessment and development for senior leaders. *Industrial and Organizational Psychology, 11*(4), 630–652.

Our List of Superstars – Participating CEOs

Company	CEO name
AAR	John Holmes
Academy Sports + Outdoors	Ken Hicks
Alurx	Julia Stewart
Anglo American	Mark Cutifani
Aternity	Bill Hewitt
Avrio AI	Nachi Junankar
Build-A-Bear Workshop, Inc.	Sharon Price John
Cardinal Innovations Healthcare	Trey Sutten
CN&CO	Carel Nolte
Craig Hospital	Jandel T. Allen-Davis
Crow Holdings	Michael Levy
Denny's	John Miller
DRDGold Limited	Niël Pretorius
Eligius Advisory, LLC	Tom O'Mara
Elite Risk Acceptances	Christelle Colman
Evlonet	Alessandro Felici

(*Continued*)

(Continued)

Company	CEO *name*
Flexible	Priya Amin
Foot Locker	Dick Johnson
Freelancer.com	Matt Barrie
Glen Dimplex Consumer Appliances	Robin van Rozen
Intellyk, Inc.	Vineet Kumar
IPA Equities	Keith Herman
Kerrits Activewear, LLC	Melissa Hubbard
Levi Strauss & Co	Chip Bergh
Lionstone Investments	Jane Page
Maryland State Bar Association	Victor Velazquez
Mascoma Savings Bank	Clayton Adams
MassChallenge	Siobhan Dullea
Maugel Architects	John Lawlor
Moonlight Therapeutics, Inc.	Samirkumar (Samir) Patel
Pacaso	Austin Allison
Panera Bread	Niren Chaudhary
PlayMonster	Tim Kilpin
Remidio Innovative Solutions	Anand Sivaraman
Ruth's Hospitality Group, Inc.	Mike O'Donnell
SA Ubuntu Foundation & Amy Foundation	Kevin Chaplin
SantaFe HealthCare, Inc.	Larry Schreiber
Satio, Inc.	Sharad Joshi
SmartBear Software	Frank Roe

(Continued)

(Continued)

Company	CEO *name*
Standard Charter Bank	Bill Winters
Target	Brian Cornell
The Athena Alliance	Coco Brown
The Swift Group	David Page
Three Square Market	Patrick McMullan
Transaction Capital	David Hurwitz
Ulta Beauty	Mary Dillon
Volk Optical	Jyoti Gupta, PhD
William Jackson Food Group	Norman Soutar
Wood River Health Services	Alison Croke
Yesware	Joel Stevenson
biotechnology firm	unnamed CEO

Endorsements

"I recommend any book by Kim Janson...to CEOs and to those who aim to be one. I've been CEO for six public companies and learned more from Kim than from any expert or consultant. She made my team better and me too. She can do the same for you."

Terry Considine, *CEO of Apartment Income REIT Corp.*

"Dr. Kim Janson is a master architect of leadership assessment and building high performing teams. Working together in two companies, she was the catalyst for managers dynamically expanding their leadership potential, which in turn sparked high velocity corporate growth. *Determining Leadership Potential: Powerful Insights to Winning at the Talent Game* delivers the ultimate blueprint for leadership and success."

Roger Snell, *CEO of Conifer*

"I have been in business over three decades, used many resources in my career, and have never had someone so effective, so quickly. Kim Janson is strong yet encouraging. She is approachable and forward thinking. Kim is helpful and effective with me as a CEO as well as anyone else on the organizational chart. I truly wish Kim would have appeared to me years ago but I'm pleased she is on the team today. We have a great foundation and high potential which I am confidant will continue to deliver outsized returns. Accordingly, I highly recommend *Determining Leadership Potential: Powerful Insights to Winning at the Talent Game.* Leadership and talent development is a never ending journey filled with unlimited potential and we all should be so lucky as to have Kim on our team."

Brad Chambers, *CEO of Buckingham Companies, Secretary of Commerce at the State of Indiana*

"Is there a business topic more important than leadership potential? Yet, for too long companies have relied on back-of-the envelope thinking. Not anymore. *Determining Leadership Potential: Powerful Insights to Winning at the Talent Game* brings deep research and practical experience together to finally lay out the key building blocks that help make leaders great. After reading this book you'll never again have to wonder whether you're assessing leadership potential effectively."

Sydney Finkelstein, *Professor at the Tuck School of Business at Dartmouth, author of the bestsellers* Why Smart Executives Fail *and* Superbosses, *and host of the podcast,* The Sydcast

"The book we have needed for decades! For the past 37 years I have worked with organizations around the world on leadership and I am so excited by the research and recommendations in this book. Companies, associations, and communities *need* better leaders and this book provides both the reason and the blueprint. Kim has distilled the concept of leadership into a tangible set of attributes that empower organizations to be intentional in their organizational development. If we are to chart a path forward that delivers on our collective promise, it will be through the methodology identified and articulated by Kim Janson."

Dave Mitchell, *President of the Leadership Difference, Inc. and author of* The Power of Understanding People

"A key element in leadership development is assessment. This important book offers a step-by-step guide for assessing and developing leaders for today and tomorrow."

Ronald E. Riggio, *PhD, Kravis Professor of Leadership and Organizational Psychology at Claremont McKenna College*

"One has to read this book carefully to use it well. It's worth it. The process of identifying and developing effective leaders is the highest priority for sustained organizational success. Authors Kimberly Janson and Melody Rawlings have produced a superb resource for doing this. This excellent book is ideal for practicing leaders and human resource professionals responsible for leadership talent management. *Determining Leadership Potential: Powerful Insights to Winning at the Talent Game* is appropriate for all sizes and forms of business, government, and non-profit organizations."

George Manning, *Professor and author of numerous books including* The Art of Leadership

"*Determining Leadership Potential: Powerful Insights to Winning at the Talent Game* provides a fresh perspective on leadership and the potential of employees to rise to the challenges and opportunities faced in today's business environment. Dr. Kimberly Janson and Dr. Melody Rawlings have documented extensive research, along with a plethora of academic references and practical tips, including quotations from 50+ leading CEOs. The book is equally relevant for academics, leadership coaches, leaders, managers, and aspiring leaders across large and small organizations to reflect on their leadership practice and become more proficient in determining leadership potential."

Catherine Mattiske, *CEO / Managing Director at*
TPC – The Performance Company

"I was intrigued when Dr. Janson reached out and thrilled when I realized I had discovered a kindred spirit. She comprehends deeply the impact of leadership on business performance, not just at the executive level, but throughout the fabric of any organization. Her work here shows a depth and breadth of understanding that will serve any leader well in their own personal journey."

Bill Hewitt, *CEO, founder, and managing member at*
Windmill Hill Advisors

"Having worked with my friend Kim as a colleague and advisor for more than 15 years, first at H.J.Heinz and then at FrieslandCampina, and having gotten so much out of her first book, *Demystifying Talent Management*, I cannot wait to benefit from *Determining Leadership Potential: Powerful Insights to Winning at the Talent Game* in my daily and dairy business life. I truly appreciate Kim for her laser-sharp analysis and inspiring coaching style."

Jan Kruise, *Senior Vice President Europe at*
FrieslandCampina

"The chief differentiator between the success and failure of any organization – be it a private company or an intelligence agency – is its ability to select good leaders and to place those people in positions where they can have the biggest positive impacts. In her new book *Determining Leadership Potential: Powerful Insights into Winning at the Talent Game*, Kim Janson takes on this crucial challenge. Combining her own deep experience in the leadership development arena with the experiences of CEOs working in a broad range of industries, Kim provides readers with a blueprint to assist executives in identifying and growing the future leaders of their organizations. Putting the right people in the right place and optimizing their opportunity to succeed ought to be a central focus of every senior leader; Kim's book helps them do so!"

Mark Kelton, *former Deputy Director for Counterintelligence at CIA National Clandestine Service*

"Janson and Rawlings have hit a home run. They've built on the sound research of Allan Church and Rob Silzer. DLP provides leaders and HR professionals a pragmatic roadmap to aid them in determining which of their talent can go far and fast."

Jim Shanley, *President at The Shanley Group, former Head of Leadership Development and Staffing at Bank of America*

"It is very difficult for me to properly describe the impact Kimberly Janson has had on our organization in a few short sentences. So simply stated, it is nothing short of profound. She has allowed my team to communicate, strategize and grow through better communication and alignment of team goals. And because of this, there is more meaning, purpose and fun going down our path."

Paul Odland, *founder and CEO of Belveron Partners*

"The author, Dr. Kimberly Janson, wants nothing less than to change the world for the better, and this book is a strong step in that direction. We need better leaders, and it starts by improving our ability to determine leadership potential!"

Mike O'Donnell, *Chairman at California Pizza Kitchen, and former Chairman and CEO of Ruth's Hospitality Group*

"Kim is a highly engaged and driven coach working to unleash our potential at Pure Development. Her book is an eye-opener and a blueprint for determining true leadership potential. The book is also a big-time reminder of the negative impact of having the wrong person in a leadership role. The chapters on personality and motivation are so very enlightening, a must-read!!"

Chris Seger and Drew Sanders, *co-founders of Pure Development*

"Dr. Janson makes a strong case for the 'burning platform' of leader selection and development. Will companies other than the Pepsis of the world have an appetite to do what must be done to 'win'?"

David F. Hoff, *COO, EASI Consult, and author of* Learning Agility: The Key to Leader Potential *and* Developing Learning Agility: Using the Burke Assessments

"Like it or not, a select group of individuals generate a disproportionate impact. These difference makers are contagious and create a positive multiplying effect on those around them. The challenge, however, is finding these high-potential leaders so that they can be positioned for future success. Janson and Rawlings have cracked the code by highlighting the vital characteristics of these rising leaders. If you are in the business of performance, you must read this book."

Michael J. Arena, *Vice President Talent at Amazon Web Services, and author of* Adaptive Space

"*Determining Leadership Potential: Powerful Insights to Winning at the Talent Game* is a game-changer when it comes to hiring, developing, and retaining top talent and maintaining a deep bench of high potential talent. The Leadership Blueprint is the first tool I have found that gives a tangible roadmap for assessing leadership potential, and it works. I have a copy of the Leadership Blueprint taped to the bottom of my computer screen as a constant reminder. This book is a must-read for all who have struggled to accurately assess leadership potential."

Jennifer Johnson, *Executive Vice President, Chief Administrative Officer and General Counsel at AIMCO*

"A must-read for every HR and talent management professional! Finding the *right* person for your company and team doesn't need to be a guessing game. Beautifully written and researched, *Determining Leadership Potential: Powerful Insights to Winning at the Talent Game* will arm you with the tools you need to identify the best leaders for each role and help your business thrive."

Marshall Goldsmith, *PhD, Thinkers50 #1 Executive Coach and New York Times bestselling author*

"Dr. Kimberly Janson's experience and wisdom in identifying leaders are distilled in *Determining Leadership Potential: Powerful Insights to Winning at the Talent Game* and is especially relevant for high growth organizations that tend to select leaders based upon on their past individual performance rather than true leadership potential. Having the pleasure of Kim's firsthand advice and counsel, this book is a must-read for high growth organizations."

Yat-Pang Au, *CEO of Veritas Investments*

"*Determining Leadership Potential: Powerful Insights to Winning at the Talent Game* is a must-read for any executive. This book addresses a core structural deficiency many organizations face today and provides a real-world road map on how we can truly elevate our 'talent game'."

Nicholas Gross, *Senior Vice President of AAR Corp.*

"The leadership blueprint is really an amazing approach to identify who are the best talent, and this book, *Determining Leadership Potential: Powerful Insights to Winning at the Talent Game*, does an amazing job of providing ideas of how to put it into action. In a moving and volatile environment, it is critical to understand how to define a talent and who is ready for big roles. It is all about ownership, self-awareness, and potential to grow."

Jacques Pradels, *Chief Sales Officer at The Kraft Heinz Company*

"Leading and building leaders in tumultuous times is never easy – the insight that Dr. Janson and Dr. Rawlings give us in this book is incredibly helpful in this endeavor. This is an insightful, well-written, and incredibly timely text. This will become a staple in my and many other people's toolkits who are tasked with leading and developing leaders."

William J. Quinn III, *DBA, Vice President of Operations, Roscom, Inc.*

"With dedicated research gleaned from a wide group of executives representing decades of leadership and leadership development, Kim Janson's book, *Determining Leadership Potential: Powerful Insights to Winning at the Talent Game*, tackles and provides insights and guidance concerning one of today's most needed, yet elusive, management qualities. If you want to improve your odds of making the right choices for people to successfully guide your company now and into the future – this book is for you."

Sharon Price John, *CEO of Build-A-Bear Workshop, Inc.*

"McKinsey and co. coined the phrase 'war for talent' in the 1990s when competition was becoming more global, the workforce was aging, and employees were willing to be more mobile. This is even more true now. Employees are in the driver's seat. This time is being called the Great Resignation or Great Reckoning. It is also a time of Great Attrition or Great Attraction. So, this book is perfectly timed. Leaders need to learn how to attract, develop, and retain talent. The authors use their extensive research to distill wisdom about determining leadership potential. This book is valuable because it can be used in a number of ways with various audiences. Each chapter has a summary of key points and a case study for discussion. There are tools and ideas that can be applied immediately. Based on interviews with more than 50 CEOs, Janson and Rawlings have identified themes and insights that should get the attention of leaders at all levels. True leadership is not about the leaders, but how well they lift up others—develop leadership potential. This is an important book to add to my (and anyone's) business library."

> **Jann E. Freed**, *PhD, Leadership Development and*
> *Change Management Consultant at The Genysys*
> *Group, and author of* Leading with Wisdom: Safe
> Advice from 100 Experts and Breadcrumb Legacy

"As a leadership consultant, trainer, executive coach, professor, and author, I've read hundreds of books on the topic of leadership, but this terrific new work by Kim Janson and Melody Rawlings takes an insightful, informative, and inspiring look at how we determine people's leadership potential in the first place. From defining basic terminology and providing an innovative framework to real-world interviews, research-backed examples, and thought-provoking case studies, this book takes a fresh look at leadership potential that will appeal both to academics and business professionals alike. In fact, I will immediately be adding *Determining Leadership Potential: Powerful Insights to Winning at the Talent Game* to the syllabi for my NYU and Columbia leadership graduate courses, as well as recommending it to all of my executive coaching clients."

> **Todd Cherches**, *CEO of BigBlueGumball, and*
> *author of* VisuaLeadership: Leveraging the Power of
> Visual Thinking in Leadership and in Life

"In a global business world containing, as the authors of this book put it, 'amazing leaders,' why do we also come across so many 'mismatched leaders' and just plain poor ones? Obviously, there's a problem here that needs to be resolved, and this book will enable that to begin happening.

The authors have researched this problem thoroughly, extracting from their research not only insights but a plan of effectual action. It's time for companies to start resolving this problem now! Read this book and learn from it...and take action!"

Ken Lizotte CMC, *Chief Imaginative Officer of Emerson Consulting Group Inc., and author of* The Expert's Edge: Become the Go-To Authority People Turn to Every Time

"'If it weren't for the people, it'd be easy,' a joking lamentation too often uttered when outcomes aren't as intended. Well, we can't assume away the challenges...and, as we know, it's the people – or more precisely the right leaders in the right roles – that enable and drive success. Sounds simple, but as Kim and Melody describe, we make it much too difficult. We are less systematic about leadership selection than about just about anything else in our business world! And, yet leadership selection is a fundamental difference maker. In Kim's characteristic manner, this book pulls back the curtain on this pervasive shortcoming, shows us the consequences, and challenges us to do better. And, because Kim is all about 'unleashing potential,' the book clearly sets forth an actionable framework to make real this mission critical work. After this, we have no excuses!"

Lisa R. Cohn, *President and General Counsel at AIR Communities*

"Most executives and HR professionals believe they know leadership potential when they see it – unfortunately they are often wrong, and the consequences of poor leadership can be devasting on the business. In *Determining Leadership Potential: Powerful Insights to Winning at the Talent Game*, Janson and Rawlings present a compelling case for change and offer a comprehensive, actionable and much needed guide for raising the bar on talent. If you truly care about identifying strong leaders for the future of your business, you need this book by your side."

Allan H. Church, *PhD, Senior Vice President at Global Talent Management at PepsiCo, Inc.*

"One of the hardest things to do for a coach is to assess the potential of their coachees and then grow and develop them to exceed the same! Dr. Janson's book outlines an effective way to approach this challenge."

Niren Chaudhary, *CEO of Panera Bread*

"Goes beyond offering a compelling case for being intentional about developing leadership potential and provides actionable insights and steps for doing so. Well-researched and full of practical examples."

Barry Z. Posner, *PhD, Endowed Professor of Leadership and Chair at the Department of Management & Entrepreneurship, Leavey School of Business, Santa Clara University, and co-author of the bestselling and award-winning book* The Leadership Challenge

"*Determining Leadership Potential: Powerful Insights to Winning at the Talent Game* is a timely examination of the alarming dearth of successful leaders. It is a well-researched and insightful study which sheds light on a proven and very practical approach for assessing leadership potential."

Julia Stewart, *founder and CEO of Alurx*

"At a time when we are struggling with the 'Great Resignation' many businesses are struggling to retain talent. Organizations must identify the right leaders who can see through the fog, lead through disruption, and provide compelling engagement for all employees. Dr. Janson and Dr. Rawlings have authored a timely and relevant book designed for organizational thought leaders."

Eugene Wilkerson, *PhD, Senior Professional in Human Resources, President of Northcentral University*

"Useful insights and practical framework for determining leadership potential (backed by science)! Dr. Janson offers a more thorough and contemporary way to examine the notion of leadership potential at various leadership levels. CEOs, executives, HR professionals, executive coaches, leadership scholars and business leaders will all benefit from the clear criteria for identifying high potential talent and recommended applications."

Tiffany Dotson, *PhD, Vice President and Head of Enterprise Learning & Development at Liberty Mutual Insurance*

Index

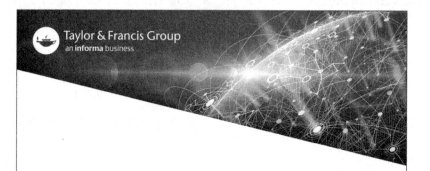

Printed in the United States
by Baker & Taylor Publisher Services